A KID'S GUIDE TO SEWING

16 Fun Projects You'll Love to Make & Use

Learn to Sew with Sophie & Her Friends

SOPHIE KERR WITH
Weeks Ringle AND **Bill Kerr**

FunStitch
STUDIO

an imprint of C&T Publishing

Text copyright © 2013 by Sophie Kerr, Bill Kerr, and Weeks Ringle

Photography and Artwork copyright © 2013 by C&T Publishing, Inc.

Publisher: Amy Marson

Creative Director: Gailen Runge

Art Director / Book Designer: Kristy Zacharias

Editor: Cynthia Bix

Technical Editors: Carolyn Aune and
Gailen Runge

Production Coordinator: Zinnia Heinzmann

Production Editor: Alice Mace Nakanishi

Illustrator: Bill Kerr

Photo Assistant: Mary Peyton Peppo

How-To Photography by Diane Pedersen of
C&T Publishing, Inc., unless otherwise noted;
Style Photography by Jim White, unless
otherwise noted

Published by FunStitch Studio, an imprint of C&T Publishing, Inc., P.O. Box 1456,
Lafayette, CA 94549

Library of Congress Cataloging-in-Publication Data

Kerr, Sophie, 2001-

 A kid's guide to sewing : learn to sew with Sophie & her friends - 16 fun projects you'll love
to make & use / Sophie Kerr, Bill Kerr and Weeks Ringle Designs.

  pages cm

 ISBN 978-1-60705-751-2 (soft cover)

1. Machine sewing--Juvenile literature. 2. Handicraft--Juvenile literature. I. Ringle, Weeks.
II. Kerr, Bill, 1965- illustrator. III. Title.

 TT712.K44 2013

 646.2'044--dc23

                    2012049281

Printed in China

10 9 8 7 6 5 4

CONTENTS

Acknowledgments

FROM SOPHIE

Thank you to Andrea, Cayla, Evan, Holly, Iris, Isa, James, Jenny, Katarina, Maria, Mary Kate, Merit, and their parents for making it possible for them to join the fun. Thank you also to the adults who helped us out—Jim the photographer and all the "kid wranglers," Gini, Judy, Kathy, Louise, Sharon, Vaishali, and Yvonne. Special thanks to our cat, Mies, for being a great model.

FROM BILL AND WEEKS

Thanks to all of the folks at C&T, especially Cynthia, Carolyn, Kristy, Zinnia, Alice, Sue, Gailen, and Amy.

We also thank all the kids and their parents, who were generous in making sure that they were where they needed to be, appropriately dressed, neatly groomed, and well rested. We are especially grateful to Mary Kate and Yvonne for making the simple variation of the *Cuddle Fleece Throw* (page 124). While we worked on this book, our dependable interns, Vaishali Chudi, Cindy Dapogny, and Vanessa Vanderzee, helped keep the studio running and the orders filled. We feel very fortunate to have such a great team of hard workers. Our "kid wranglers" were essential to keeping the kids on track, making sure they were having fun, and guiding them in their sewing. Thank you to Judy Chaffee, Kathy Durochik, Louise Gates, Yvonne Malone, Sharon Quintenz, and Gini Williams, who have cheered us on so faithfully for more than a decade.

We feel so fortunate that professional photographer Jim White makes time in his schedule to do photography for our books and magazine. We have done many, many photo shoots with Jim, but having him work on this book was especially meaningful for us. Jim has known Sophie since she was three, has been her soccer coach at times, and is the dad of one of her closest friends (who is also one of our kid models). As a dad, Jim was so great with all of the kids, putting them at ease and understanding how uncomfortable it is to be smiling in 103°F heat. We could never have gotten such wonderful shots without him.

Thanks in advance to all of the patient adults who will help kids make projects from this book and will pass on a love of sewing.

Weeks Dye Works (no relation to author Weeks Ringle) generously supplied the wool and embroidery floss for *Backpack Decorations* (page 86). Everyone who worked with these beautiful wools asked where to purchase them. Ask if your local fabric shop carries Weeks wools. If not, you can find a list of retailers on the Weeks Dye Works website, listed in Resources (page 142).

Thanks also to the Bilyk family and the Oak Park Public Library for letting us shoot on their premises.

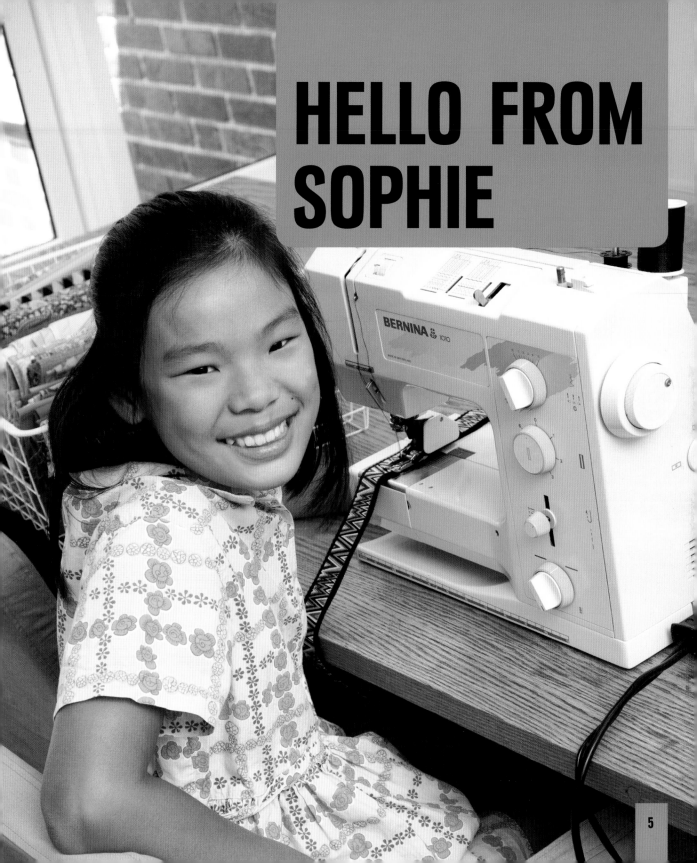

HELLO FROM SOPHIE

Hi! My name is Sophie, and I am eleven. I started playing with fabric and sewing when I was three. Lately I've been learning more about sewing. With help from my family and friends, I've been making a lot of projects. I want to share with you what I learned.

In this book you will learn the basic skills you need for sewing. If sewing interests you, you will learn more skills with every project you make.

Throughout the book, you will see special notes from me. These give you tips about the projects and help you with the hard parts from a kid's point of view. For example: One hard part about sewing any project is that you have to make sure the fabric is not slipping around. So don't sew too *fast*!

I had a lot of fun picking fabrics, making the projects, and seeing them finished. My favorite part about fabric is the many different designs and colors. Everyone can find something they like to use. The project I enjoyed most was *Backpack Decorations*. Which one do you think you will like best? My favorite colors are pink, purple, red, and yellow. When I go shopping I like to get florals, paisleys, and other patterned fabrics in those colors. What are your favorite

colors and types of fabric? When I finish a project, I am satisfied because it is done and I can use it. I hope you will be proud and satisfied with your projects, too.

You can make sewing fun! It's fun to sew with friends. Have a sewing day when you invite some friends to come sew with you at your house. Instead of giving goody bags filled with candy at your birthday party, you could make a couple of things like the hairband or the zippered pouch from this book. Then one day you could all wear them to school and be matching—or different.

So, have fun sewing the projects in the book. But if you're doing a project after school, make sure you do all your homework *first*, so you don't get in trouble!

Happy sewing!

A WORD FROM WEEKS AND BILL (MOM AND DAD)

Weeks remembers wanting to sew a pair of pants when she was five years old. As a tween, she sewed an overly complicated stuffed animal for her best friend's birthday and made clothes in home economics class in junior high. But there were no patterns or projects written for kids that would help them learn skills one project at a time.

When Bill was a child, his mother kept her sewing machine in his room. Its mechanical complexity lured him. By age eight he was taking it apart and putting it back together. Along the way, he learned to sew. His first project was an ill-fated attempt to sew a kite.

It didn't occur to him that the leftover piece of corduroy he used would be far too heavy to fly!

We encouraged our daughter, Sophie, to sew when she was just three years old. One of us would hold her on our lap and operate the pedal while she pushed the fabric through the machine.

In writing this book as a family, our hope is to open up a new world to kids. Sophie sewed all or most of each project, and we adapted patterns to make sure that kids could be successful on their own or with an experienced helper. We have included projects for many skill levels, so the book will "grow" with the sewist, offering new challenges as kids gain more skills with age and experience.

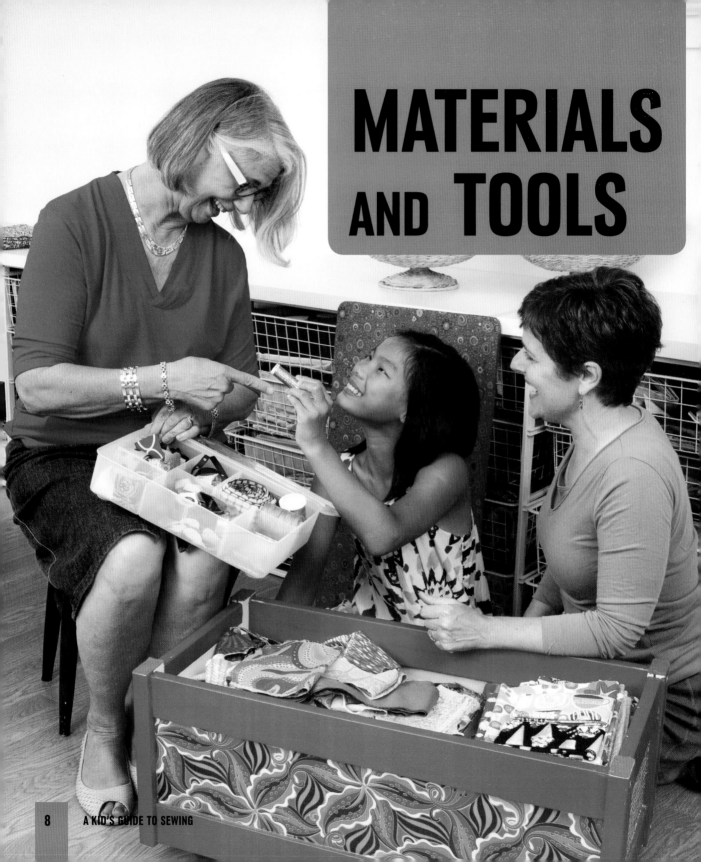

MATERIALS AND TOOLS

Exploring Fabrics

Choosing fabrics for your project is one of the most fun parts of sewing. You get to pick colors, patterns, and prints that you love. But understanding how to choose the *right* fabric for a project is also an important part of successful sewing. You might really like a certain fabric in the store or online. But if it isn't the right type of fabric or the right weight for your project, it may not be a good choice. Using the wrong type of fabric will make any project harder. You may be disappointed in the result. Here are the main categories of fabric that we used in this book.

Quilting-weight cotton

Cotton flannel

Upholstery-weight fabric

WOVENS

Woven fabrics have just a little stretch. They vary in weight, from lightweight to very heavy.

Quilting-weight cotton

Many of the projects in this book—such as the patchwork part of *Cuddle Fleece Patchwork Throw* (page 122), *Gini's Tiered Skirt* (page 108), and *Quilted Place Mats* (page 94)—were made using quilting-weight cotton prints. Most of these fabrics are 100% cotton. Some shops carry blends of polyester and cotton.

Cotton flannel

Flannel is a soft fabric that has been brushed so it feels good against the skin. We made *Sleepover Bag* (page 66) with flannel so it would be soft and could also be used as a pillow. There are different weights for flannel. A lightweight flannel would be good for a warm winter version of *Gini's Tiered Skirt*. You could also use flannel for a pillow or pillowcase. It wouldn't be good for a lunch bag, though, because it would be hard to laminate and keep clean.

Upholstery-weight fabric

This is a heavier-weight printed or solid fabric that is a little stiffer and sturdier. We used upholstery fabric for *Reversible Messenger Bag* (page 82) and *Simple Pillow* (page 46). We used vinyl for *Zippered Tote* (page 132), but upholstery-weight fabric would also have been a good choice. You may also hear the term "home dec fabric." Home dec is short for "home decor." Home dec fabric includes all kinds of fabric used for furniture, curtains, pillows, and so forth. The heaviest home dec fabrics are considered upholstery fabrics. When a project calls for a heavier fabric, you can also use corduroy, velvet, or denim.

Canvas

We used a heavy canvas for the bottom and zippered pocket of *Sleepover Bag* (page 66) to make it long-wearing. Canvas is stiffer than many fabrics, so it's hard to use for projects that have lots of small pieces. The seams get too bulky. Canvas is often made out of cotton and is also known as "cotton duck." When the canvas is made out of nylon, it's called Cordura.

Canvas

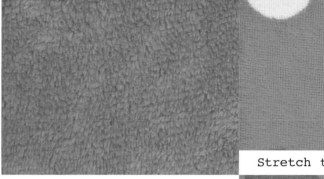

Cuddle fabric

Stretch terry cloth

CUDDLE FABRICS

Duck, Duck, What?

You may be asking, "Why do they call it cotton duck?" Does it have anything to do with ducks? Cotton duck got its name from doek—*a fabric used for the pants and coats of sailors from the Netherlands.* Doek *is the Dutch word for linen canvas, a durable fabric that blocks the wind. The term "cotton duck" has been used in English to refer to heavy cotton woven in the same way as* doek.

The cuddle fabrics we used for *Washable Pet Bed* (page 50), *Cuddle Fleece Scarf* (page 54), and *Cuddle Fleece Patchwork Throw* (page 122) are all knits. Some cuddle fabrics have a lot of stretch in one direction but not in the other. For the throw, we sewed woven fabric (quilting cotton) to the back side of the cuddle fabric. This kept it from stretching and made it easier to sew. The edges of cuddle fleece shed a lot, so it's a good idea to overlock stitch the seams when possible. (You will learn about overlocking on page 32.) Like regular fleece, cuddle fleece is made of synthetic (human-made) fibers. But cuddle fleece is softer and feels plush. Some cuddle fleece feels almost like fake fur. There are various brand names for cuddle fleece, such as Minky.

Stretch terry cloth

You probably have regular terry cloth in your home. It's the thick fabric with the tiny loops used in towels and washcloths. When it's a towel, it's a woven fabric. But sometimes you'll see a knit terry cloth, such as the one pictured in *Pool Cover-Up* (page 102). You can tell it's a knit if it stretches a lot. Terry cloth absorbs a lot of water, which makes it a good choice for the pool cover-up. But it would be a bad choice for a lunch bag, because it would pick up every spill at the lunch table!

KNITS

Knits are made to stretch. The stretch is helpful in some projects but can make other projects a real mess. So it's important to use knits for the right projects.

Vinyl

Felted wool

Insulating fabric

OTHER MATERIALS TO KNOW

Felted wool

Felted wool is soft and thick. It's great for projects like *Backpack Decorations* (page 86), because you can cut interesting shapes from it without hemming the edges. Regular wool ravels just as cotton does, but the process called "felting" uses hot water to shrink the wool. Once it's felted, you can cut the wool and the edges won't ravel. Some people take old 100% wool sweaters with holes in them and felt them in the washing machine and dryer. Some fabric stores carry a lighter weight of felted wool in small sheets. But we used ready-made felted wool for *Backpack Decorations*. "Felted wool" generally refers to knit wool that has been shrunk. "Wool felt" is the term used for wool that has been pressed into sheets rather than knitted or woven into fabric.

Vinyl

Vinyl is a fabric made from plastic that has been bonded to a knit or woven fabric. Vinyl is often a thick, heavyweight fabric that is sometimes made to look like leather. It is water resistant and sturdy, so it's a good choice for tote bags and seat cushions. We used a vinyl that looks like leather for our *Zippered Tote* (page 132). It's easy to wipe off and resists rain and snow.

Insulating fabric

For *Insulated Lunch Bag* (page 116), we included an insulating layer covered by a nylon lining fabric to keep cold food chilled. Insulating fabrics are stiff, which also helps the lunch bag sit up. Usually one side is best for the outside of a bag, and the other side insulates best when it's on the inside. Be sure to follow directions with insulating fabric.

Webbing

Webbing

Webbing can be made of cotton or nylon. It is a good material to use for belts and for straps on tote bags. We used it as a base for *Fancy Ribbon Belt, Two Ways* (page 72).

Fancy Ribbon Belt

Fabric Basics

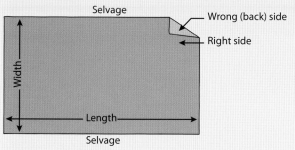

RIGHT SIDE *of the fabric is the side with the pattern printed on it. The wrong side refers to the back.*

SELVAGES *are the finished edges of the fabric.*

WIDTH *is the distance from selvage to selvage.*

LENGTH *is the distance from one cut edge to another, along the selvage.*

Fabric comes in different widths. Quilting cottons are usually 42″–44″ wide. Upholstery-weight fabric is most often 54″ wide, but it comes as wide as 60″. Most knits are anywhere from 36″ to 60″ wide. Make sure you know how wide your fabric is, because this will affect how much of it you will need for a project.

"Fat quarter" is the term used to describe a ½-yard piece of fabric that has been cut in half down the center, between the selvages. A standard ¼-yard cut would be 9″ × 42″, but a fat quarter is 18″ × 21″ because it's cut differently. Quilting cotton is often sold in fat quarters, but most other types of fabric must be bought with standard selvage-to-selvage cuts.

Buttons

Beads

NOTIONS

"Notions" is the term for other items used in sewing.

Buttons

Buttons can be made out of plastic, metal, wood, clay, or even shells. Some buttons can go in the washing machine, while others have to be dry-cleaned. Be sure to check the care instructions before you buy buttons. Also check to make sure they are the right size for the project. Most buttons are labeled in both inches and millimeters, such as "¾″ (19mm)."

Beads

Beads can be made from plastic, metal, wood, glass, or clay. When buying beads, check that the hole in the bead is big enough for the needle you plan to use.

Fancy ribbons

Ribbons come in different widths, so check how wide the ribbon should be for your project. Ribbon is usually sold by the yard, but some craft stores sell small rolls of ribbon that are precut to a certain length. Be sure to read the length on the roll as well as the width, to make sure you get enough. Most ribbons are machine washable, but read the label on the ribbon holder to be sure before you take it to the cutting table. Once ribbon has been cut, it can't be returned.

Embroidery floss

You can use embroidery floss to add decorative hand stitching to your projects. Most embroidery floss is made from cotton. Some floss is thicker than others, so choose carefully for each project. Crewel yarn, which is usually made from wool, looks like embroidery floss. Embroidery floss is better for projects that will go in the washing machine, such as *Embroidered Pillowcase* (page 78). But crewel yarn would be fine for projects made of wool, such as *Backpack Decorations* (page 86).

Embroidery floss

Thread

There are so many types of thread that it's hard to know the difference between them. Usually thread at the fabric store is sorted by use. General sewing thread will be in one place. Then there will be a separate area for quilting thread or heavy-duty thread. These heavier threads would be great for sewing a button on a coat, but too thick and heavy for sewing lace.

Most threads are made of cotton or polyester. Cotton doesn't melt with heat like polyester can, but polyester is stronger than cotton. You'll find some thread that is all cotton, some that is all polyester, and some that is a blend. The blends combine the best qualities of each. Usually it's a good idea to try to match the thread to the fabric you'll be sewing.

Thread

Choose a thread that is the same color as the main color in the fabric. Or, if the fabric is a print, try to match the least bright color in it. At the store you'll be able to unwind a small amount of the thread to hold up against the fabric. Be sure to do this because thread looks different on the spool than it does as a single strand. There are also special kinds of thread, such as invisible thread and elastic thread, which you'll learn how to use in some projects.

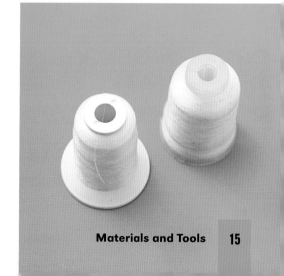

Zippers

Zippers

Zippers are made with either plastic or metal teeth. Either one is okay to use. Ordinary zippers come in many lengths and thicknesses. You can get them 7″ long, 8″ long, and even longer. Ordinary zippers do not come apart at the base. "Separating zippers" are the ones used for coats. These come apart when they're unzipped so you can take the coat off. Some zippers are called "invisible zippers" because they seem to "disappear." This means that when they are closed you don't see the zipper teeth. The zipper projects in this book use ordinary zippers.

D-rings

D-rings are a useful notion for making a custom-fitting belt. You use these instead of a belt buckle. When buying D-rings, be sure to double-check that the width of the D-rings matches the width of the webbing you'll be using.

D-rings

Purse handles

For *Zippered Tote* (page 132), we used ready-made nylon purse handles with metal parts. Purse handles come in many lengths and sizes. If you plan to wear the bag over your shoulder, make sure the handles are long enough.

Purse handles

Laminating sheets

It's easy to laminate fabric for small projects like *Insulated Lunch Bag* (page 116). You just use laminating sheets (also called "iron-on vinyl") from the fabric or craft shop. It usually comes in a 15″-wide roll. Iron-on laminating won't last as long as ready-made laminated fabric. But it's useful to know how to laminate fabrics yourself. When laminated fabric gets dirty, hand wash it or just wipe it clean.

Laminating sheets

Elastic

You can buy elastic by the yard at the fabric store or in precut packs. It comes in a lot of widths and thicknesses. We thought a thinner elastic would be good for *Gini's Tiered Skirt* (page 108). A thick elastic is better for heavier fabrics and can also keep a waistband from rolling.

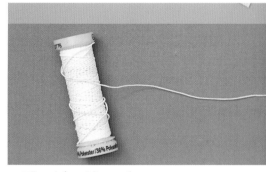

Elastic

Elastic thread

Sophie loved using the elastic thread! It's fun to watch the flat fabric bunch up so quickly. Elastic thread usually just comes in three or four colors such as white, black, red, and navy. It's made of a very thin piece of elastic with cotton wrapped around it. Usually you only use elastic thread in the bobbin. You use regular thread as the top thread. Be sure to follow the directions that come with the elastic thread. The directions will usually tell you not to use your sewing machine's bobbin winder. The winder stretches the elastic, so it won't sew well. If you follow the directions and wind it by hand, it should be fine. It's always a good idea to experiment on a scrap of fabric before you sew the final project.

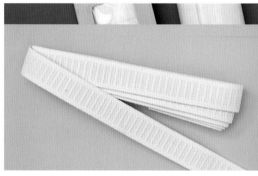

Elastic thread

Ponytail holders

Elastic usually comes by the yard and is cut in long strands. When you need a small loop of elastic, the ends can be hard to hide. For *Insulated Lunch Bag* (page 116), we used a ponytail holder to solve that problem.

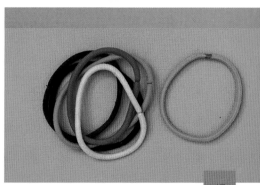

Ponytail holders

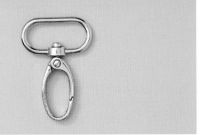

Backpack clips

Double-sided fusible tape

Backpack clips

There are lots of different names for these clips. Some people call them "fobs" and others call them "swivel clips" or "backpack clips." Whatever you call them, they are ideal for attaching things to backpacks and purses.

Double-sided fusible tape

Fusible tape helps to keep two materials together while you're sewing. It's easy to iron on and comes in different widths. The handiest is the ¼" tape. This tape is helpful when you're learning how to sew with zippers, and when you are trying to sew trim onto any material. Two brands to use are HeatnBond Quilters' Edge (by Therm O Web) and Steam-A-Seam (by The Warm Company).

Using Fusible Tape

Double-sided fusible tape has two sides. One is a little bit sticky, and the other has paper on it. Follow the instructions that come with the tape. Place the sticky side on the project and the paper side up. Put a scrap of fabric underneath and on top of the project, to keep the tape from sticking to the iron or the ironing board. Gently press the iron on top to melt the fusible tape onto the project fabric. Once it's cool, peel the paper off and pin the piece of fabric to whatever you want it to stick to. Then press it again with the iron.

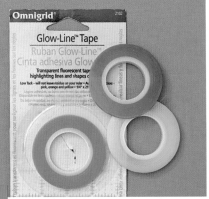

Marking tape

Marking tape is handy to use if you are cutting many pieces of fabric that are the same size. You can place the pieces of tape on your ruler or cutting mat to mark where to cut. Be sure to remove them when you're done so you don't get confused on your next project.

Marking tape

Tools You'll Need

You will need a few simple but important tools for sewing. To find out where you can get some of them, see the listings in Resources (page 142).

Iron

safety first

Be careful with irons! They can burn you if you accidentally touch the metal surface. They are dangerous if you forget to turn them off, and they will most likely break if you drop them on the floor. Most irons have a steam option, which only works when there is water in a little tank inside the iron. Steam is very helpful when you're sewing. Always ask the owner of the iron how it works and how to add water when it's empty. Be sure to turn off the iron and stand it on its end when you're done.

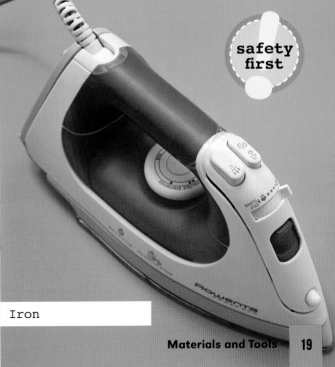

safety first

Iron

Magnetic pincushion

Magnetic pincushion

When someone at our sewing studio drops a bunch of pins, no problem! We just wave the magnetic pincushion over the pile, and the pins seem to jump onto it. As with any magnet, be sure to keep the pincushion away from electronics such as computers, because magnets can interfere with the memory of some devices.

Marking pens/chalk

There are many ways to mark fabric for sewing. One is using water-soluble pens. They look like regular markers, but the mark comes out with water. Another is chalk pencils that can be used like a regular pencil, but the chalk marks brush off easily. We like the Clover chalking tool because it makes a smooth and very thin line that's easy to see on most fabrics.

Needles

It's a good idea to have a variety pack of needles. You'll need different sizes of needles for different projects. The thicker the needle, the bigger the hole it will leave in the fabric. So try to use the thinnest needle you can manage. You'll need larger needles for embroidery floss and smaller needles for regular thread.

Marking pens/chalk

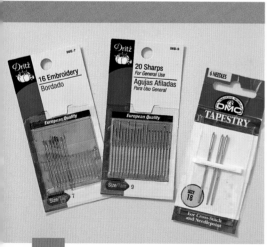

Needles

Pins

Did you know that there are different kinds of pins? Some are short; others are long. Some have tiny metal heads; others have plastic balls on the ends. We like flower head pins because they are long and easy to grasp. Tailors like shorter pins because they make it easier to see how fabric drapes. Also, smaller pins are less likely to poke someone trying on clothes with pins in them. Think about which kind would be easier for you to use before you buy any.

Pins

Rotary cutter

Rotary cutters look like small pizza cutters. Be careful because they are dangerously sharp! Always use the rotary cutter with an adult who knows how to use it. Don't forget to close the blade when you're finished cutting, and always wear a safety glove to protect your other hand while you cut. Use the rotary cutter with a ruler and a mat for cutting straight or curved lines quickly. The rotary cutter can cut through several layers of fabric at once. But if you stack more than four layers, the fabric may slide around. Then the cuts won't be accurate. For more about cutting safely, see Be Safe with Rotary Cutters (page 35).

Rotary cutter

Ruler

Cutting rulers come in many widths. Some have plastic edges that make them easy to slide along the cutting mat. Others have a piece on top that is easy to grasp. Choose one that you think will be easiest to control.

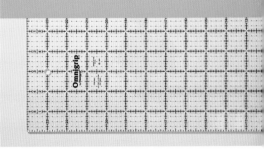

Ruler

Cutting mat

If you are buying a cutting mat to use with your rotary cutter and ruler, get one that's at least 24″ × 36″. Almost every project in this book needs a large mat to be able to cut safely and accurately. Look for a mat that's "self-healing." These mats stay smooth after each cut. Always store the mat flat. Don't leave it in a hot car, or it can get permanently warped.

Cutting mat

Measuring tape

Safety glove

Measuring tape

Rulers are good for cutting and measuring fabric when it's flat. But to measure anything that isn't flat, you'll need a measuring tape. For example, use a measuring tape to measure your body for clothing.

Safety glove

There are many types of safety gloves for rotary cutters, but most are sized for adult hands. If the glove is too big, it will be harder to grasp the ruler safely. So make sure you buy a glove that fits. We found a cut-resistant glove for small hands, and it's listed in Resources (page 142).

Scissors

You've probably been using scissors since you were little. But did you know that scissor blades get dull from cutting paper? That's why you should have a separate pair of scissors for cutting fabric. We use a rotary cutter for cutting out fabric, but scissors might be easier for you. There are hundreds of different kinds of sewing scissors available. We use a large pair and a small pair the most. The large one is good for cutting fabric. The small one is great for trimming threads or snipping corners with good control.

Seam ripper

The seam ripper is a sewist's best friend. Look for one that fits nicely in your hand. Always point the seam ripper away from you because it is very sharp. Be sure to store it with the cap on for safety.

Bicycle clips

Bicycle clips (for pants), also called "quilter's roll clips," are handy to use when you're sewing something large. Roll up the sides of the project and slip the clips around the fabric. That will make it easier to handle during sewing.

Beeswax

Beeswax is very helpful for hand sewing. Slide your thread through the beeswax container before you sew. The beeswax coats the thread so it doesn't get tangled as easily.

Binder clips

To hold two pieces of fabric together before you sew them, you will usually use pins. But pins will leave small holes in laminated fabrics, vinyl, leather, and some other materials. There are two tricks to avoiding this. First, you could pin inside the seam allowance so the hole won't show in the final project. The other option, which Sophie thought was really fun, is to use binder clips. The clips come in several sizes. They hold thick pieces of vinyl or projects with lots of layers together really well. You can also use them to hold together all of the parts of a project if you need to clean up before you're finished.

Seam ripper

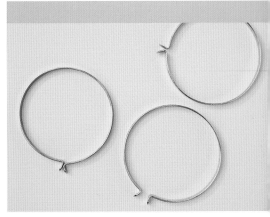

Bicycle clips

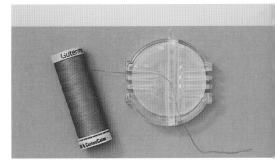

Beeswax

Binder clips

YOUR SEWING MACHINE

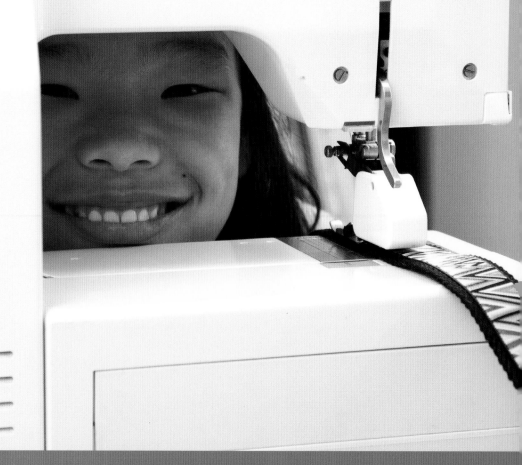

Getting to Know the Parts

A sewing machine manual probably doesn't sound very exciting. But every machine is different. Reading the manual will tell you how to use and take care of your machine. It will show you how to thread the machine, how to change the bobbin, when and where to oil it, and how to change the feet and needles.

Let's look at the parts found on every sewing machine.

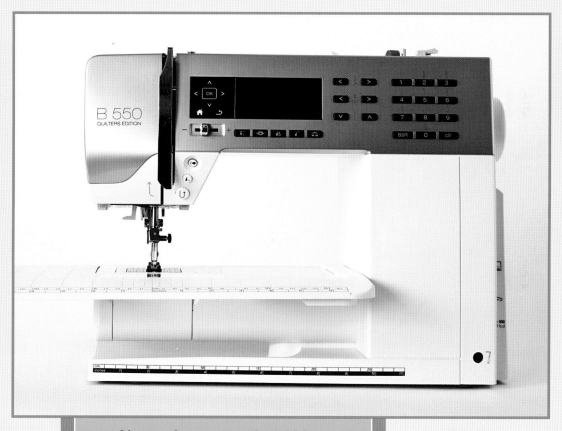

Reading the manual will tell you how to use and take care of your machine.

Needle

Your manual will show you how to change the needle. You'll be changing the needle when it breaks or when you need a different needle for a specific task. For example, when sewing thick vinyl, it's smart to use a thicker needle so it doesn't break. A needle made for sewing leather would be a good choice. There are special needles for knits, jeans, and many other fabrics. But most of the time you'll be sewing with a "universal" needle. A universal needle works for most fabrics other than the heavy-duty fabrics or projects with lots of layers.

Thread holder

This part holds the spool of thread in place. Each sewing machine has its own threading sequence—the path that the thread follows from the spool to the needle. If this path is not followed carefully, the stitches may not be even, or you may get knots on the front or back of your project. Threading your sewing machine the right way is a great skill to have, and one of the first to master.

Bobbin

The bobbin is the small spool of thread that sits inside the machine and makes the stitches on the back of whatever you are sewing. It's a good idea to use the same type of thread in the bobbin and on top. The manual will show you how to wind the bobbin on your machine.

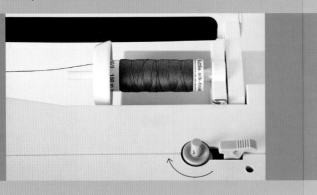

Bobbin case

On some machines, the bobbin goes inside a small case before it is placed into the machine. On some machines you load the bobbin from the front. On others, you load it under the needle plate. Pay close attention to the diagram in the manual for loading the bobbin into the bobbin case and placing the bobbin case into the machine. Many machines also have an ideal sewing tension for the bobbin. Ask your sewing machine technician to show you how he or she tests the tension on the bobbin.

Bobbin race

The bobbin (and its case if your machine has one) is inserted into a space that allows the bobbin to turn. This space is called the "bobbin race." It should be cleaned every time you change the bobbin. You can use a small brush, a cotton swab, or our home-made cleaner, described under Clean Machine (page 34). Don't stick pins or anything else in the bobbin race that might scratch it. In some machines, the bobbin race needs to be oiled. Check the owner's manual or ask a sewing machine technician if this is a good idea for your machine.

Presser foot

The presser foot and the feed dogs work as a team. The presser foot presses the fabric down so the feed dogs below will move the fabric forward to make room for the next stitch. There's a lever at the back of the sewing machine used to raise and lower the presser foot. Always raise and lower the presser foot gently. Don't let it slam down on the needle plate.

Feed dogs

The feed dogs are the ridged parts that come up through the needle plate to advance the fabric. In some machines they can be raised or lowered. But for all of the projects in this book, you can keep them up.

Needle plate

This is the flat metal plate under the needle and presser foot. It is sometimes called a "throat plate." It has an opening for the feed dogs and a hole for the needle to pass through. Most needle plates have lines marked on them. You can use these lines to guide the fabric while sewing.

Specialty feet

Some sewing machines come with just one presser foot. But most have the option to buy specialty feet that make some sewing jobs easier. Many machines have a special foot for sewing zippers, and some have a foot for using an overlock stitch to finish fabric edges. There's a foot used for quilting called a "walking foot." Some are built into the sewing machine and others you buy separately. Not every machine can use a walking foot. But if yours does, it can be helpful when sewing thick layers together. Check your manual for the feet that are available for your machine.

Light

Most sewing machines have a light bulb that helps you see what you're sewing. Like all light bulbs, these sometimes burn out. Check your manual to learn how to replace the bulb. Be sure to let the bulb cool off before you try to change it.

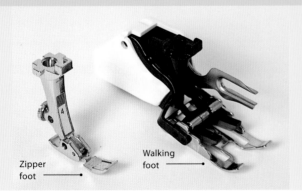

Zipper foot

Walking foot

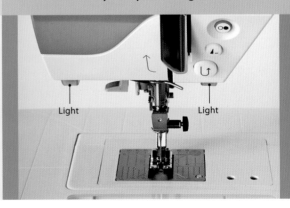

Light

Light

Stitch length setting

On some machines, there is a knob or button that adjusts the length of the basic stitch. On others, there is a screen you touch to change the length. If you change the length for a special task, some machines automatically reset it when they are turned off. But if yours doesn't, remember to change the stitch length back to normal before you turn the machine off.

Stitch width setting

This sets the width of the stitch for a zigzag stitch or for an overlock stitch.

Needle position setting

On some machines, you can move the needle to the left or right with this setting. For example, when using a zipper foot, you usually need to move the needle to the far left or right to line up with the correct hole in the zipper foot. Pay attention and set the needle position correctly when you change feet. This will avoid breaking needles.

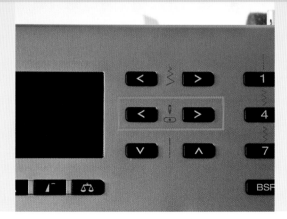

Hand wheel

The hand wheel is the large round piece on the right side of many machines. It allows you to move the needle up and down by hand. It's helpful to use if you get thread jammed in the machine. You will also want to move the needle by hand when you are tacking the end of a zipper. It will help you avoid breaking the needle.

Pedal

The pedal sits on the floor and controls the speed of the needle as it goes up and down. If you push the pedal hard with your foot, the needle goes faster. It might seem fun to push the pedal to sew faster. But ripping out stitches that aren't in the right place wastes a lot of time and is boring. Taking your time to do things right the first time makes sewing more fun. Don't worry—you'll get faster with time and practice, while still keeping control of your stitching.

Tip

It's a good idea to have a sewing machine technician your family can trust to tune up your machine regularly and to fix it if anything goes wrong. This person can also help you understand how your machine works and the best way to use it. Ask your parents if it's okay for you to get to know the technician, so you can ask him or her for help and advice.

Learning to Use Your Machine

To use your sewing machine, you will need to learn a couple of simple stitches and some basic machine maintenance.

BASIC MACHINE STITCHING

Before you start sewing a project, practice the stitches you'll be using. To avoid wasting fabric, ask if it's okay to practice on some clean rags or fabric scraps.

For the projects in this book, you need to know how to sew a straight stitch and a zigzag stitch. For some projects, an overlock stitch is helpful for finishing fabric edges. If your sewing machine doesn't have an overlock stitch, you can use a zigzag stitch instead.

As you sew, you need to line up the edge of the fabric with a guide. You can use the edge of the presser foot (if it's the width you need) or one of the lines marked on the needle plate (page 28). So if the project calls for a ½″ seam allowance, find which line on the needle plate is ½″ from the needle. Use that line as your guide.

Straight stitch

This is the stitch you will use most of the time. To sew a seam with a straight stitch, pin two pieces of fabric together. They should have their right sides together and their edges lined up. Place the fabric under the presser foot, with the edge of the fabric along either a line on the needle plate or the outside edge of the presser foot. Gently guide the fabric along as you push the foot pedal. When you open up the fabric, you won't be able to see the stitches very easily. Read Backtacking (page 33) to see how to secure the beginning and end of the seam.

Zigzag and overlock stitches

Most machines have a zigzag stitch. This is a wide stitch that is useful for sewing the edges of fabrics so they don't ravel. Some machines also have an overlock stitch. You may have seen this on the seams inside of T-shirts and other knit clothes.

The overlock stitch also helps to prevent raveling. Check the sewing machine manual to learn how to set your machine for zigzag stitching and to see if it can do overlock stitching.

Topstitching

On the hems and pockets of most jeans, you can see a line of stitching close to the edge. Sometimes the thread is a different color than the fabric. The designer wants you to notice the topstitching, which becomes a style element. Topstitching is different from stitching a seam, because you can see the stitches when you're finished. So it's good to take your time and be careful, so your stitching will look neat.

Rolled hem

Let's say that you want to sew some cotton napkins, and you don't want the raw edges of the fabric to fray every time you wash them. You'll need to finish the edges. The best way is to use a rolled hem. Fold the edges to the inside by ¼", and fold again another ¼". Press and then topstitch the edge. That's a rolled hem.

Backtacking

When you backtack, you sew a few stitches forward, then back, then forward again at the beginning or end of a seam. This keeps the stitching from pulling out easily. Most sewing machines have a button or lever that lets you reverse the direction of the stitches. You should backtack when you know a seam will be pulled a lot, such as the side seams in a tote bag. When you're sewing a tote bag together, it's a good idea to backtack at the beginning and end of every seam.

MAINTAINING YOUR SEWING MACHINE

Most problems with your sewing machine can be avoided if you take good care of it. One of our sewing machines is 23 years old, but it runs like new. That's because we clean it often, oil it when needed, and have a technician tune it up every year or so. The most important thing is to read the manual and talk with a sewing machine technician. Below are some general tips, but an expert can help you understand what's best for your machine.

Keep it clean!

Every time you change the bobbin, make it a habit to brush the lint out of the bobbin case and the bobbin race. If you don't have a small brush for cleaning your machine, you can make one as described in Clean Machine (at right). Don't use a can of "spray air" to clean it! It can push lint farther into the machine.

Place a small drop of clear sewing machine oil on the bobbin race if your manual recommends it. Use just a drop or two. If you put too much oil in the race, it might leak onto your project—so be careful. A fine-tipped oil dispenser makes it easy to control.

When it's time to get your machine serviced, ask the technician to show you the best way to keep your machine clean and oiled.

Unless you are sewing several times a week, it's a good idea to keep a cover on your sewing machine to keep out dust. Keep spools of thread in a pretty glass jar with a lid or in a sewing box so they don't bring dust into the inside of the machine either.

Clean Machine

To make a handy tool for cleaning your sewing machine, cut a plastic drinking straw in half as shown. Fold a pipe cleaner in half and stick the ends into the straw, leaving the folded end of the pipe cleaner sticking out. This makes a great tool for cleaning your sewing machine. The pipe cleaner will pick up lots of lint, but it won't scratch the inside of your machine. Note: Pipe cleaners are often called "chenille stems" in craft stores.

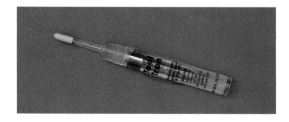

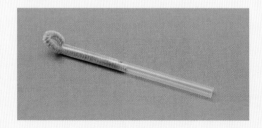

THE BASICS OF SEWING

Safety First!

safety first

Safety is the most important part of sewing. Review this section with an adult. Make sure you understand how to cut and sew safely before you start any project.

BE SAFE WITH ROTARY CUTTERS

In Tools You'll Need (page 19), we mentioned the dangers of cutting with a rotary cutter. Professionals close the blade of the rotary cutter *every time* they put it down. Never leave a rotary blade exposed! It's easy to get distracted and forget to close it. Meanwhile, someone bumps into it or a pet brushes up against it—and someone will get hurt. Some rotary cutters close automatically. One of these might be a good choice for a new sewist.

PAY ATTENTION

Pay attention when you're cutting and sewing! Don't cut when you're tired, when you're deep in conversation with a friend, when your favorite song is blaring, or when you're in a hurry. Those are the times when you're more likely to hurt yourself. Do all your cutting when you're alert and can focus. The same goes for sewing. You'll make fewer mistakes.

Planning Your Project

GET READY!

It's easy to get really excited about a project and want to get started right away! Sewing is like cooking, though. You want to read through all of the instructions and make sure that you have everything you need before you start.

GET HELP IF YOU THINK YOU MIGHT NEED IT

If you're sewing for the first time or doing something new like sewing a zipper or sewing with elastic thread, pay extra careful attention to the instructions. Consider asking a friend or family member to help you or answer questions.

START SMALL

The projects in this book are organized from the easiest to the most challenging. Ideally you'd start with the easy projects and learn one skill at a time. But if you want to sew *Zippered Tote* (page 132) as your first project, ask an experienced sewist to make it with you. He or she can do the tricky parts, and you'll learn a lot as you watch.

BE REALISTIC ABOUT TIME

If you want to make something at the last minute, choose a simple project. When I was in middle school I wanted to make my best friend a yellow and green stuffed hippo. It was a really complicated project, and I started it the night before my friend's birthday party. It was so frustrating to find that it was too big a project to do in the time I had. I was disappointed when I had to ask for help to finish it in time.

In her special Sophie Says notes, Sophie tells how long it took for her to make many of the projects in this book. That should help you figure out what you can make in the time you have.

CHECK YOUR STITCHES AS YOU SEW

Our sewing machine repairman told us that 80 percent of the problems with stitches happen in the first 6 stitches. So every time you start a new seam, check the front and back to make sure the stitching looks good.

Learning the Basics of Sewing

CUTTING

If you are cutting with scissors, use a pencil or marking pen to mark the cutting line. Be sure to use sharp scissors, because dull scissors cannot cut fabric very easily. If you're cutting with a rotary cutter, hold the cutter in the hand you use to write. Wear a safety glove on your other hand. Use the edge of a ruler to guide your cutting. Always cut away from your body, and always close the rotary cutter when you're done. (For more on cutting safety, please see Safety First!, page 35.)

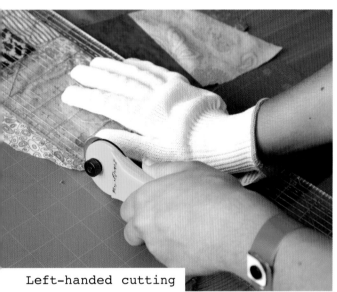

Left-handed cutting

Right-handed cutting

PINNING

The best way to pin for machine sewing is to pin perpendicular to the raw edge. That way you'll see the pins, and they will be easy to remove while you are sewing. Avoid sewing over the pin. This may break the needle, which can be dangerous as well as frustrating.

THREADING A NEEDLE

It's easiest to thread a needle if the end of the thread has a clean cut. It's also a little easier if the end of the thread is moist, so the fibers lie flat and stick together. So among sewists, it's okay to stick the end of the thread in your mouth to wet it, and then smooth it with your fingers.

Needle Threader

Some sets of hand-sewing needles include an odd-shaped tool called a needle threader. To use it, stick the thin wires through the eye of the needle if you can. When the wire V comes out the other side, put the thread through the triangle between the threader and the needle. Now pull the threader out of the eye of the needle. This should bring the thread though the eye as well. This tool doesn't work on needles with tiny eyes, but it works well on most other needles.

SIMPLE HAND SEWING

Most hand sewing is done with a single strand of thread. If you're sewing on a button or something that needs a strong stitch, use a double strand and knot both strands together.

Cut a piece of thread about the length of your arm. It's best not to use a super long piece because it will get tangled more easily. Running the thread through a beeswax holder before sewing will help to prevent tangles.

Tying a Knot

These drawings show you how to tie a knot in a single or double strand of thread.

SEAM ALLOWANCES

Seam allowance

The seam allowance is the space between the raw edge of the fabric and the seam. Clothing patterns sometimes call for that to be anywhere from ⅜″ to ⅝″. Most clothes are sewn with a ⅝″ seam allowance. People who make quilts usually sew with a ¼″ seam allowance. Check the pattern carefully before you start sewing. Make sure you sew with the right allowances, or your project will end up too small or too large.

PRESSING

"Pressing" means ironing something flat with an iron. Set the temperature of the iron to match the fabric you are using. For example, there's usually a cotton setting or a wool setting that's the right temperature for that material. When directions say to "press the seams," sometimes you can press both sides of the seam allowance to one side. Other times it's better to press them open. Follow the instructions, because each pattern may be different.

Pressed to one side

Pressed open

Embroidery

Embroidery is the art of using colored threads to decorate fabrics with pretty stitches and designs. There's a whole world of embroidery designs and stitches to learn either online or through books at your local library. We give you just two projects with embroidery on them. But you could actually embroider designs on most of the projects in this book!

Embroidered Pillowcase (page 78)

Embroidery floss has six strands of thread twisted together. You can use all six strands, or you can separate them. To do this, cut a length of floss and gently pull it apart to get the number of strands you want. The more strands you use, the thicker your embroidery will be.

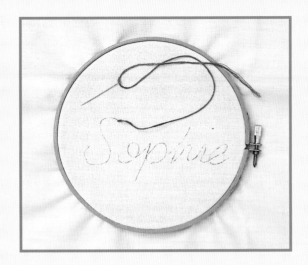

Once you choose a design to embroider, you can trace it onto the fabric by taping it up on a window. The light will shine through so you can see the lines.

Then you will put the fabric into an embroidery hoop to stitch it. Additional instructions are in Embroidered Pillowcase (page 78).

If you're doing embroidery for the first time, here are some basic stitches used in this book.

Running stitch

Backstitch

1.

2.

3.

4.

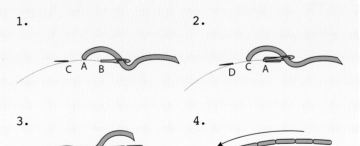

Blanket stitch

1.   2.

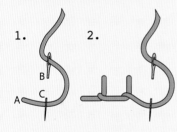

3.

French knot

1.

2.

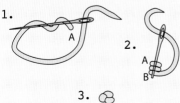

3. ∂

MEASURING YOUR BODY

For both *Pool Cover-Up* (page 102) and *Gini's Tiered Skirt* (page 108), you'll need to know some important measurements of your body. Below is a worksheet you can use to write your measurements. When you make the cover-up or the skirt, you'll find additional measuring instructions for those particular projects.

Name:

Date of measurements:

Bust:

Waist:

Hips:

Length from waist to knee:

Length from armpit to knee:

Sophie Says...

When making clothes, you'll need to measure your body. Place the measuring tape directly on your body. If you measure your waist over a bulky sweater, for example, it won't be accurate. Have a parent, a sibling, or a friend actually do the measuring. Be sure to stand up straight. That will get you the correct measurement. Take each measurement twice to make sure you didn't make any mistakes. Write the date next to your measurements. Remeasure each time you make anything you'll wear. You might have grown since you took the last measurements.

Oops! How to Deal with Mistakes

Everyone makes mistakes cutting or sewing, even professionals. When that happens, here's the most helpful thing to figure out: Is the mistake small enough that it won't make a difference? Or is the mistake going to make more and more problems later? For example, if you cut a piece of fabric ¼˝ too big, you can trim it down right away, and the problem is fixed. But if it's ½˝ too *small*, the pieces will never fit together quite right. If you can make the whole project ½˝ smaller, that might be a good solution. If not, you're probably better off starting over again.

In general, the more accurately you cut, the easier the project will be to sew.

Here are some common mistakes, and advice on how to fix them.

☐ **A piece is too big**   Cut it down to the correct size right away.

☐ **A piece is too small**   If it's more than ¼˝ too small, recut it. Or you might be able to make the whole pattern smaller. For example, making a tote bag ½˝ smaller is not a problem. But cutting the elastic for a skirt waistband 1˝ too short will make the skirt uncomfortable.

☐ **The seam allowance is less than ¼˝ after sewing**   Take out the stitches with a seam ripper, and restitch the seam. You'll probably end up with a hole if you don't.

☐ **The seam allowance is too wide after sewing**   See if it will affect the overall project. When sewing her *Cuddle Fleece Patchwork Throw* (page 122), Sophie ended up with a slightly wider seam allowance for every strip. Over 38 strips, that little bit added up to the quilt being 10˝ shorter than she had planned! We added extra strips to make it the length she wanted, so it wasn't a problem. But she was surprised how a little tiny bit extra in the seam allowance over so many seams added up to a big number.

☐ **Your stitches look uneven or messy**   The sewing machine is probably not threaded correctly. Check the manual and rethread the machine. Rip out the bad stitches, because they will make more problems later.

projects
FROM BEGINNING
TO ADVANCED

Some of the sixteen projects in this book are fast and easy. Some are still easy, but take more time. Others require more skill, but are pretty fast to make. Then there are the most challenging projects, which take skill *and* require time. We've arranged the projects in this order—according to how hard they are and how much time they take. When possible, Sophie has noted in her sidebars how long it took her to complete the project. So that should help you figure out if it's the right project for your skills and the time you have to work on it.

simple pillow

A pillow is a great first project because it's small and simple. *And* you can make it in a fabric and color that goes with your room. Choose a fabric you love that is also machine washable. You'll probably want to wash it if it's going to get a lot of use. Just don't let it get damaged in a pillow fight!

Finished size: 20″ × 20″

MATERIALS

- ☐ ¾ yard of 54″-wide home dec fabric, corduroy, denim, or any heavyweight fabric
- ☐ Matching thread
- ☐ 20″ × 20″ square pillow form

TOOLS AND SUPPLIES

- ☐ Sewing machine
- ☐ Iron
- ☐ Scissors or rotary cutter and mat
- ☐ Straight pins
- ☐ CD to use as a pillow corner pattern

Tip

You can use plain or print fabric. If you're using fabric with a large motif, you may need to buy extra so you can center the design on the front.

CUTTING

From home dec fabric, cut:

- ☐ 1 pillow top piece 21″ × 21″
- ☐ 2 pillow bottom pieces, each 13½″ × 21″

Sophie Says...

Once you have the materials, this is a fast project. You could even make it after school. You can make the pillow fancier if you want to add pom-poms or other kinds of trims. It's easy to see how you could customize the pillow for a friend's room. Pay attention sewing around the curves of the corners.

SEWING

1. Place the right side of 1 bottom piece face down. Fold 1 long edge ½″ over to the wrong side. Press.

2. Fold the edge over ½″ again. Press. Now you have a rolled hem.

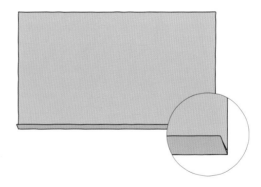

3. Topstitch along the fold. This will keep the edges from fraying.

4. Repeat Steps 1–3 for the second bottom piece.

5. With right sides facing each other, align the outer edges of the top piece and the 2 bottom pieces. The hemmed edges of the bottom pieces will overlap in the middle. Pin the layers together on all 4 sides.

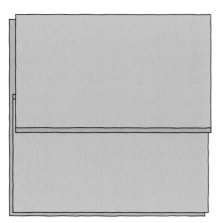

6. Using a CD as a pattern, fit the edges of the CD against 2 sides of a corner and trace the curve. Do this on all 4 corners. Cut out the curve. Throw away the leftover square corner pieces. This curve will keep the corners from sticking out in the finished pillow.

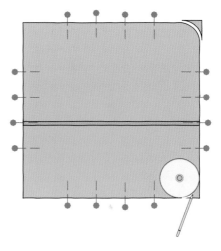

7. Using a ½˝ seam allowance, sew around the edges.

8. Overlock or zigzag stitch the edges to prevent fraying.

9. Turn the pillow cover right side out. Put the pillow form in it. When you want to wash the cover, it's easy to take out the pillow form.

washable pet bed

Our furry friends deserve a warm and soft place to sleep. This simple project is a great "gift" for your cat or dog. It can even be a fun and washable play surface for rabbits and pocket pets. It's so simple to make, and you can use our directions to make it in different sizes. You might even want to make more than one!

MATERIALS

- ☐ ¾ yard of 56″-wide fleece, cuddle fleece, or other soft, washable fabric

- ☐ Matching thread

- ☐ 15″ × 17″ piece of 2″-thick foam (available in some craft stores, or can be cut to size)

Tip

If you're using fabric with a large motif, you may need to buy extra so you can center the design on the front.

TOOLS AND SUPPLIES

- ☐ Sewing machine

- ☐ Scissors or rotary cutter and mat

- ☐ Straight pins

CUTTING

From fabric, cut:

- ☐ 1 bed top piece 18″ × 20″

- ☐ 2 bed bottom pieces, each 11½″ × 20″

Sophie Says...

You can adapt the pet bed to the size of your pet. Choose the right size foam so your pet can actually sleep on it. For example, if you have a Great Dane, you'll need a really big piece of foam. You can figure out how much fabric you'll need using the explanation in Customize Sizing for Your Pet (page 52). Choose a fabric that you can throw in the washing machine and that maybe even looks good with your pet! The pet bed is a lot like Simple Pillow (page 46), except it has "gussets." Gussets are seams that you sew across the corners. They shape the pet bed cover like a shallow box, so you can put a thick, square piece of foam inside. I used a 2″-thick piece of foam for our cat's bed. So the gussets had to be 2″ so it would fit.

It's easy to get the foam in and out of the cover so you can wash it. If you want, you could embroider your pet's name on the cover.

Customize Sizing for Your Pet

With a little math, you can make this design fit larger pets. Choose a piece of foam that best fits your furry friend. Measure the thickness (T), the width (W), and the length (L).

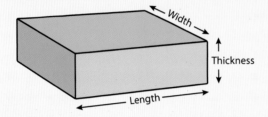

The measurement of the top piece will be:

$(W + T + 1)$ inches wide by $(L + T + 1)$ inches long

You'll need 2 back pieces, each cut:

$$\frac{W + T}{2} + 3 \text{ inches wide by } (L + T + 1) \text{ inches long}$$

Follow the steps for making the smaller bed. But for Step 5, you'll need to sew across the point that is the same width as the thickness of the foam. For instance, if the foam is 4″ thick, measure down to where the seam would be 4″ across, and sew the gusset there.

SEWING

1. Hem the back pieces. If you're using a knit fabric such as regular fleece or cuddle fleece, fold 1 long end of each back piece under 1″. Finish the raw edge using a zigzag stitch, and topstitch the folded edge in place. If you're using a woven fabric, fold under a long end of each back piece ½″. Fold it ½″ again to make a rolled hem. Topstitch.

2. With right sides facing each other, line up the outer edges of the top and bottom pieces. The hemmed edges of the bottom pieces will overlap in the center. Pin the layers together on all 4 sides.

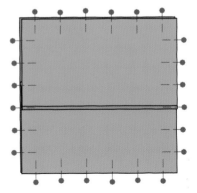

3. Using a ½″ seam allowance, sew around the edges.

4. To make the first gusset, put your hand inside the bed cover and fold a corner flat to form a triangle as shown. The side and bottom seams should be lined up. Pin together.

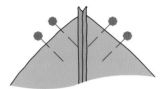

5. Find the point where the bottom of the triangle measures 2″ across (1″ on either side of the seam), and sew.

6. Trim off the triangle ½″ away from the seam as shown.

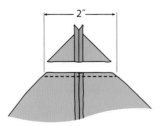

7. Repeat Steps 4–6 for all the corners.

8. Turn right side out. Insert the foam cushion. The cushion is easy to remove when you need to wash the cover.

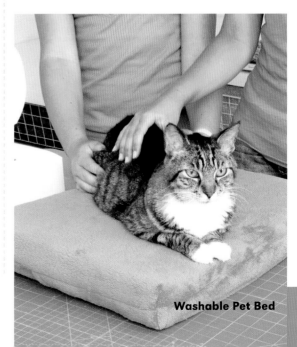

cuddle fleece
scarf

Finished size: 6″ wide × 60″ long (approximately)

Even if you don't live where there's a lot of winter snow, it's always nice to have something soft and warm against your neck. Making the scarf is so simple and fast that you could even make one for each of your siblings or friends as gifts. Cuddle fleece usually comes in 60″ widths, so it's the perfect size for scarves.

MATERIALS

- ☐ ½ yard of 60″-wide cuddle fleece
- ☐ Matching thread

TOOLS AND SUPPLIES

- ☐ Sewing machine
- ☐ Scissors or rotary cutter and mat
- ☐ Straight pins
- ☐ Chalk or water-soluble marker
- ☐ Measuring tape

Tip

Cuddle fabrics can be thin or thick. The thicker ones are warmer, but the thinner ones are easier to sew. Most are 60″ wide. If you want the scarf longer, you can cut 2 pieces the same width and sew them together end to end. If you want it shorter, just trim it to the desired length before you measure for the points. You can also place trims in the seams as you sew the angled ends.

Sophie Says...

It was a lot of fun to make this scarf. I made the whole thing in less than an hour. Cuddle fleece is very messy and sheds a lot. You'll want to clean up with a vacuum cleaner as you cut. It's also a good idea to clean the area around the sewing machine bobbin after you're done. The final product is warm and soft. You can wear it to school, around town, or even when you're just hanging out with friends.

CUTTING AND SEWING

Use a ⅝″ seam allowance for this project.

1. Cut 2 pieces 7¼″ wide. Cut them selvage to selvage, which is about 60″, depending on the exact width of your fabric.

2. With right sides together, pin along each of the long sides but not the ends. This illustration shows just the ends.

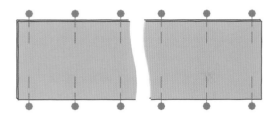

3. Sew each side using a ⅝″ seam allowance so you have a tube that's sewn on both sides.

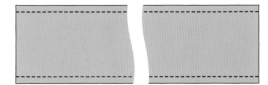

4. Lay out the scarf flat and cut off the selvages (about 1″ on each end).

5. Get the water-soluble marking pen or chalk. Draw a parallel line ⅝″ from an end of the scarf. Mark the center of the line. Next mark a point 5″ from the end of the scarf on the seam line of each side. Draw a line from the center point to each side point.

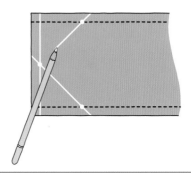

6. Sew along each of the angled lines.

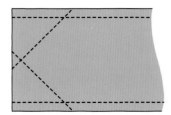

7. Draw a line ⅝″ away from the angled seams and trim along the line.

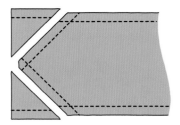

8. Repeat Step 5 on the other end.

9. Sew along *just 1* of the 2 angled lines. Leave the last line unsewn so you'll be able to turn the scarf right side out. Trim ⅝″ from both the sewn and unsewn lines.

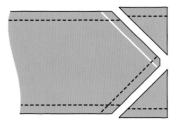

10. Turn the scarf right side out. It's helpful to use a chopstick or the eraser end of a pencil on the inside of the scarf to help poke out the pointed end.

After you've turned the scarf inside out, tuck the unsewn edges in so there's a ⅝″ seam allowance.

11. Topstitch the open side closed, backtacking at each end of the stitching line.

hairband

After Sophie made her first hairband, she began wearing it almost every day. In addition to being cute, it's an easy way to keep your hair off your face. Although it's a small project, there are lots of steps. So this isn't a project you want to make in a hurry or when you're tired. Once you've made it the first time, though, it gets much faster.

MATERIALS

- ☐ 1 piece of cotton quilting fabric 13″ × 13″ (you could use a fat quarter)

- ☐ 1 piece of 1″-wide elastic, 8″ long

- ☐ Matching thread

TOOLS AND SUPPLIES

- ☐ Sewing machine

- ☐ Iron

- ☐ Scissors or rotary cutter and mat

- ☐ Safety pins

- ☐ Straight pins

- ☐ Large paper clip

CUTTING

From fabric, cut:

- ☐ 1 piece 9″ × 13″ for top

- ☐ 1 piece 2¾″ × 12″ for band

Tip

There are two pieces to the headband, the top and the band. You can use the same fabric for both or you can use two different fabrics that look good together. The illustrations show the top and the band in two different colors so the pattern is easier to follow. But you can use just one fabric as shown in the photo.

Sophie Says...

The hairband looks simple, but it takes more time to make than you'd think. It has a lot of steps, but I made it in about one hour. If you don't have much of your favorite fabric, make a practice one with some other fabric that you like before making your final hairband.

It would be fun to have all your friends make hairbands out of the same fabric so you all can be matching. They could be good party favors for a sleepover.

SEWING
Make the top

1. With the right side of the 9″ × 13″ piece facing down, fold its top and bottom edges in ½″. Fold in ½″ again. Press flat.

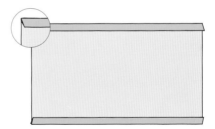

2. Topstitch along the inside of the folded edges to make a rolled hem.

Make the band

1. The band is a tube with a piece of elastic sewn into it. Fold the 2¾″ × 12″ band fabric in half lengthwise, with the right side facing in. Press.

2. Sew ¼″ from the long edge.

3. Turn the tube right side out. There's a neat trick to doing this. Pin a safety pin through 1 side at 1 end of the tube. Push it back into the tube and push it through to the other end, bit by bit.

4. Press the tube flat, keeping the seam at the edge.

5. Put a safety pin through the end of a 1″ × 8″ piece of elastic. Slide it into the tube, from left to right, until the unpinned end of the elastic is almost even with the left-hand edge of the tube.

6. Pin the left-hand end of the elastic and the end of the tube together. The safety pin end will only be partway through the tube. Sew across the end ¼″ from the left edge to anchor the elastic.

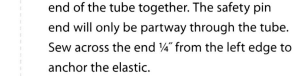

7. Scrunch the fabric tube down the elastic and pin the right-hand end of the tube and the elastic together. Remove the safety pin. Sew across the end ¼″ from the edge.

8. Stitch down the center of the tube for about 1″, so enough of the band is behind the presser foot that you can grab onto it in the next step.

9. Using your left hand to hold the end of the band behind the presser foot and your right hand to hold the end nearest you, stretch it taut. At the same time, sew straight down the middle of the band. Slowly advance the band as you sew, while keeping it fully stretched. This step keeps the elastic from twisting in the tube.

Assemble the parts

1. With the right side of the top piece facing up, center the elastic band on the left-hand short edge. Pin.

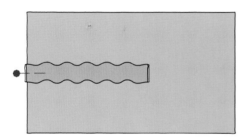

2. Fold the lower half of the top piece to the center and back 3 or 4 times. (This is called "pleating.") If it goes a bit past the center that's okay, too. It doesn't have to be exact. Press the pleats flat.

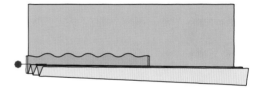

3. Fold the upper half the same way. If it ends up overlapping the bottom folds a bit, that's fine. Press these pleats flat.

4. Place a paper clip ¾″ in from the left-hand edge to hold the pleats flat and the elastic in place. Sew across the end ¼″ from the edge. Sew again on top of the same stitching line to hold it secure.

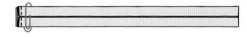

5. Open up the pleats and pull the elastic to line up the right-hand edges of the pleats and the elastic band. Clip or pin in place, and sew across and back ¼″ from the edge.

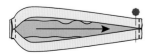

6. This last step feels like a bit of magic. Pull the elastic band out and turn the fabric right side out—and it's ready to wear!

zippered pouch

Once you've made one of these cute and easy pouches, you'll want to make a lot more to stay organized at school and at home. Sewing in a zipper may seem difficult the first time, but using fusible tape makes it a lot easier. You can change the size of this pouch to hold almost anything. You just have to find a zipper that's long enough! For details about how to make a different size pouch, turn to Changing Pouch or Pocket Size (page 71).

Finished size: 7½″ × 7½″

MATERIALS

- [ ] 2 squares of fabric 8″ × 8″
- [ ] 7″ zipper
- [ ] Matching thread
- [ ] ¼″-wide double-sided fusible tape, such as Steam-A-Seam (optional)

TOOLS AND SUPPLIES

- [ ] Sewing machine
- [ ] Iron
- [ ] Zipper foot for the sewing machine (optional)
- [ ] Straight pins

Sophie Says...

This pouch was fun to make because I got to put in a zipper. I had never done a zipper before. Using fusible tape was a good idea for beginners like me. The tape makes sure the zipper doesn't slip around.

You can choose a fabric that has one big design on it, like the large butterfly on mine. Or you can choose fabric with a little design that will be repeated all over the bag, such as a floral, a paisley, or a plaid. If you have a big design, try to center it. You could even use two fabrics, so each side is different. You can choose a zipper that matches the fabric, or a zipper that adds a new color. Add a fancy bead to the zipper pull so it's easier to open and looks pretty.

When you make the bag, make sure to use a chopstick to poke out the corners from the inside so they look neat.

Attaching a Zipper

If you have a zipper foot for your machine, it will be easier to sew close to the teeth of the zipper when you are attaching it to the fabric. If you don't have a zipper foot, the teeth make it hard to keep the zipper from slipping around when you sew. In that case, try using ¼″ fusible tape such as Steam-A-Seam to keep the fabric in place.

1. *Cut 2 pieces of fusible tape the same length as the zipper.*

2. *Place the right side of the zipper facing up. Attach a piece of tape, sticky side down, on each cotton edge of the zipper. Using a warm iron, iron on the tape.*

3. *Peel off the paper strip. Center and pin the top edge of 1 piece of 8″ × 8″ fabric, face down, on the outside edge of the zipper as shown. Press into place.*

4. *Repeat Steps 1–3 for the second side of the zipper.*

For more details about using fusible tape, see Using Fusible Tape (page 18).

SEWING

You can fuse or sew the zipper in place. To fuse it, follow Attaching a Zipper, Steps 1–3 (page 63); then skip ahead to Sewing, Step 3 (below).

1. Open the zipper halfway and lay it facing up (so you can see the zipper pull). Center the top edge of 1 piece of 8″ × 8″ fabric face down on an outside edge of the zipper. Pin it in place.

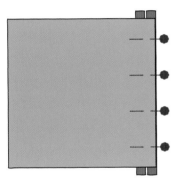

2. If your sewing machine has a zipper foot, put it on and adjust the needle position, according to your manual. Sew the fabric to the zipper using the zipper foot. Sew as close to the zipper teeth as you can. When you get to the zipper pull, if it's in your way, slide it down the zipper and finish the seam. If you don't have a zipper foot, sew as close to the zipper as you can.

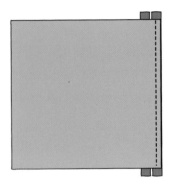

Tip

A zipper foot, unlike a regular sewing machine foot, has a cutout on the edge, instead of in the center, for the needle. On most machines, you have to move the needle position over to the edge, or it will sew right into the middle of the metal foot and break the needle! If you have a sewing machine that does not allow you to move the needle position, check your manual's instructions for using a zipper foot.

3. Fold the fabric back over, and press it flat. Topstitch close to the edge of the fold.

4. Repeat Steps 1–3 for the second side of the zipper.

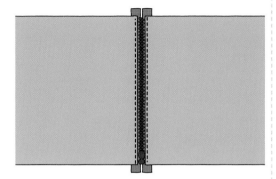

5. Open the zipper. Then fold the pouch with the right sides facing each other. It will look inside out. Line up the side and bottom edges, and pin. Sew ¼″ from the edge around all 3 sides. Make sure to backtack at the beginning and end to reinforce the stitching.

Remember to open the zipper before you sew all of the seams so you'll be able to turn the bag right side out in Step 7.

6. Zigzag around the raw edges on all 3 sides to prevent fraying.

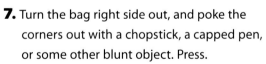

7. Turn the bag right side out, and poke the corners out with a chopstick, a capped pen, or some other blunt object. Press.

sleepover bag

Even though sleepovers usually last less than 24 hours, you have to take a lot of stuff! This simple drawstring bag holds everything you'll need and has the option to add a zippered pocket as well. You can make the whole bag out of one fabric, or make the bottom section from a contrasting fabric like the one shown here. Once you've made this drawstring bag, you'll be able to make smaller ones for extra changes of clothes, shoes, or even some games.

Finished size: 20″ × 27″

MATERIALS

For basic bag:

☐ 1 yard of fabric for
the bag

☐ 1½ yards of cord for
the drawstring

☐ Matching thread

For bag with contrasting bottom:

☐ ¾ yard of fabric for top of the bag

☐ ¼ yard of contrasting fabric for
the bag bottom

☐ 1½ yards of cord for the drawstring

For optional pocket:

☐ ¼ yard of fabric for pocket front and back

☐ 8″ zipper

☐ Matching thread

☐ ¼″ double-sided fusible tape such as
Steam-A-Seam (*optional*)

TOOLS AND SUPPLIES

☐ Sewing machine

☐ Iron

☐ Scissors or rotary cutter and mat

☐ Pinking shears or pinking blade for
the rotary cutter (*optional*)

☐ Straight pins

☐ Safety pin

☐ Zipper foot (if available)

Sophie Says...

*You can use the sleepover bag at a
friend's house. You can also take it
along when you go camping or to an
overnight scouting event. I like the idea
of customizing your own bag. You could use
ribbon or rickrack to decorate the bag.*

CUTTING

*If possible, cut fabric with a pinking blade or pinking
shears so the edges won't ravel very much.*

For basic sleepover bag, cut:

☐ 1 piece of fabric 29″ × 42″

For bag with contrasting bottom, cut:

☐ 1 piece 25″ × 42″ for the top of the bag

☐ 1 piece 5″ × 42″ for the bag bottom

For optional pocket, cut:

☐ 1 piece of fabric 1¼″ × 8½″ for pocket top

☐ 1 piece of fabric 3½″ × 8½″ for pocket bottom

☐ 1 piece of fabric 4½″ × 8½″ for pocket back

SEWING
Make the pocket (*optional*)

1. First make the pocket front. With the closed zipper facing up, center the 1¼″ × 8½″ piece of fabric face down on the edge of the zipper. Pin in place. If your sewing machine has a zipper foot, put it on and adjust the needle. Sew the fabric to the zipper using the zipper foot.

2. If the zipper pull is in your way, slide it down and finish the seam. If you don't have a zipper foot, sew as close to the zipper as you can or use fusible tape instead. For help, see Attaching a Zipper (page 63).

3. Fold the fabric over, and press it flat. Topstitch just beside the fold.

4. Repeat Steps 1–3 to sew the 3½″ × 8½″ piece of fabric to the other side of the zipper.

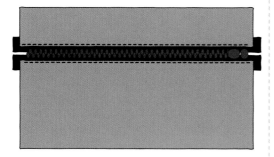

5. Open the zipper. Pin the 4½″ × 8½″ pocket back face down on the completed pocket front, right sides together. Sew around all 4 sides ¼″ from the edge.

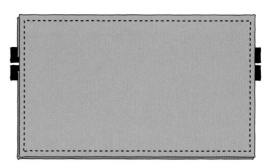

6. Turn the pocket right side out and press. Set aside.

Make the bag

1. If you're making the basic bag, skip to Step 2. If you're making the version with the contrasting bottom, place the bottom band and the top part of the bag right sides together with the long edges aligned. Stitch them together, using a ½˝ seam allowance. Press the seam to the side.

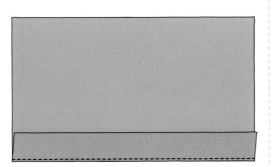

2. Turn the short ends of the bag piece under by ¼˝. Press. Zigzag over the raw edges you just pressed.

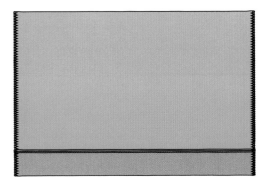

3. With the fabric face down, fold the top edge over 1˝ toward you, and press. Using a zigzag stitch, stitch over the raw edge. Backtack at the beginning and end of the stitching. This will make a channel for the drawstring.

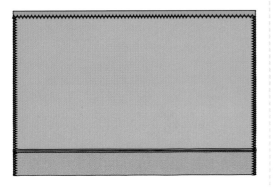

4. Turn the fabric right side up. Pin the zippered pocket in place, 10˝ from the top and 6˝ from the right-hand edge. Using a zigzag stitch, sew the pocket to the bag on all sides. Be careful not to sew into the zipper's teeth and break your needle!

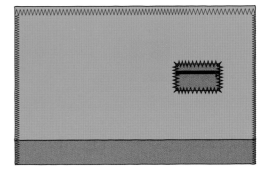

5. Push a safety pin through the end of the cord and fasten the pin. Feed the pin and cord through the channel and out the other side. Knot each cord end.

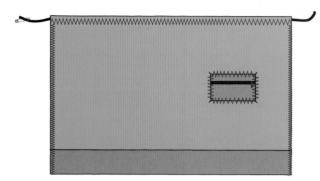

6. Fold the bag in half with right sides together. Pin the sides. Starting at the bottom, sew the sides together ¼˝ from the edge. Stop before you get to the drawstring channel. Backtack to reinforce the seam. Knot the cord ends together.

7. Turn the bag right side out.

Changing Pouch or Pocket Size

Zippered pouches or pockets can be made any size as long as you have a zipper that's the right length. The pocket on the sleepover bag has its zipper on the side. The pouch in Zippered Pouch *(page 62) has it on the top. Decide on the size pouch or pocket you want to make, and then find a zipper at least that length.*

If the zipper is a little too long, you can shorten it. You just need to sew a new zipper stop, which will keep the zipper pull from coming off the end of the zipper. Mark the length you need on the zipper. Set your machine's zigzag stitch length to zero, with the width as wide as possible. At the mark, stitch over the top of the zipper several times by turning the hand wheel. Carefully cut off the extra part of the zipper, about ¾˝ beyond the new, sewn zipper stop.

CAUTION! *Sewing near or over zipper teeth is tricky because if the needle hits the metal teeth, it can break. To avoid this, manually turn the hand wheel to create the stitches. If the needle starts to hit the metal teeth, just slide the zipper over a bit, letting the needle slide between the teeth.*

fancy ribbon belt

two ways

If you've never seen any of the fancy ribbons that are available, you are in for a treat. There are ribbons with animals, sports themes, flowers, and a lot of different patterns. We used D-rings to fasten the belt. But there are many different kinds of buckles and clasps to choose from. You can find all of them in a fabric store. This is a pretty fast project if you use the fusible tape and sew carefully when zigzagging the ribbon to the webbing. You can make the belt two ways—one-sided or reversible, for double the style! To see the reversible option, turn to *Reversible Belt* (page 76).

MATERIALS

Read the Tip (below right) about the materials before you buy the things on this list.

- ☐ Cotton or nylon webbing*

- ☐ Cotton or nylon ribbon, a bit narrower than the webbing**

- ☐ D-rings to fit the webbing width

- ☐ ¼″ double-sided fusible tape, such as Steam-A-Seam

- ☐ Invisible thread

  * To figure out how much webbing you need, measure your waist and add 10″. For help, see Measuring Your Body (page 42).

  ** For a one-sided belt, buy ribbon at least 10″ longer than the webbing. For a reversible belt, buy 2 ribbons, each 1″ longer than the webbing.

TOOLS AND SUPPLIES

- ☐ Sewing machine

- ☐ Scissors

- ☐ Leather or jeans needle

- ☐ Straight pins

- ☐ Liquid seam sealer, such as Fray Check (by Dritz), *or* a knife and access to the stove if the ribbon or webbing is nylon

Sophie Says...

Make sure that the D-rings you buy are the right size. In the fabric store, they might be with the webbing supplies. You might also find them with the purse-making supplies.

There are two ways you can make the belt. One is reversible and the other is one-sided. The reversible one is a little trickier, because you have to sew very carefully. It's a little stiffer to use because there are more layers. There aren't many steps, so it's a quick project. Be sure to sew carefully though.

Have a grown-up help you prepare the ribbon and webbing (if it's nylon) so it doesn't fray.

Using the fusible tape keeps the ribbon from slipping around. That makes it a lot easier to sew.

Tip

The webbing, ribbon, and D-rings need to work together. Make sure to buy all the materials together at the same time. The ribbon has to be narrower than the webbing so you'll have room to sew it on. The D-rings need to be sized for the webbing. For example, if you want to use a ¾″-wide ribbon, you could get 1″ webbing and 1″ D-rings. If you want to use a wider ribbon, look for wider webbing and D-rings.

PREPARING THE MATERIALS

1. Measure your waist, and cut a piece of webbing that is 10″ longer than your waist measurement.

2. Cut the ribbon (or ribbons). For a 1-sided belt, cut the ribbon 10″ longer than the webbing. For a reversible belt, cut each ribbon ½″ longer than the webbing. Trim any frayed ends.

3. Get help from an adult to seal the ends of the webbing or ribbon using heat. With a potholder, hold a pocketknife over a flame on the stove or a candle until it's very hot. Gently touch the cut edge of the ribbon or webbing to the hot knife. The heat will seal the ends. This method is neater than using liquid seam sealer.

If you don't want to use heat, you can also sew across the cut ends of ribbon or webbing with a small zigzag stitch.

If you prefer to use liquid seam sealer, use a small brush or cotton swab to apply it to the cut ends of the ribbon or webbing.

SEWING

One-sided belt

Tip

Most people feed a belt through belt loops with their dominant hand. Usually it doesn't matter which way you put on your belt. But it does matter in this project, if you're using ribbon with a "directional" design, like Sophie did in hers. If you're using a ribbon with a pattern that looks wrong when it's upside down, be sure to figure out which way you put on your belt before you sew the ribbon on the webbing.

1. Apply a strip of double-sided fusible tape down the center of 1 side of the webbing. With a warm iron, fuse the tape according to the instructions on the package.

2. Peel the paper backing off the tape. Center the ribbon on the webbing, and pin. The ribbon is longer than the webbing, so it will hang off the webbing at the end that will not have the D-ring. If your ribbon has a "directional" design (if it can't be used upside down), read the Tip (at left) first.

3. Using a pressing cloth and a warm iron on top of the ribbon, fuse the ribbon to the webbing.

4. Cut a piece of fusible tape just a bit shorter than the length of the overhanging ribbon. Pin and fuse the remaining part of the ribbon to the back of the webbing.

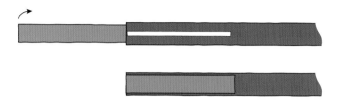

5. Using invisible thread for both top and bobbin threads, sew each edge of the ribbon to the webbing. Stitch slowly and consistently with a small zigzag, making sure to catch the edge of the ribbon with each stitch.

6. Slide the other end of the webbing through both of the D-rings. Wrap the end back so there's a loop of webbing around the rings.

7. Pin the end of the webbing to the back side of the belt, allowing enough room that the rings can move a bit. Using a jeans or leather needle, sew the loop closed, backtacking at the beginning and ending of the stitching.

Reversible belt

1. Apply a strip of double-sided fusible tape down the center of a side of the webbing. With a warm iron set on nylon or synthetic, fuse the tape according to the instructions on the package. Leave the paper strip on.

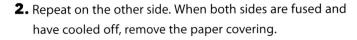

2. Repeat on the other side. When both sides are fused and have cooled off, remove the paper covering.

3. With right sides together and using invisible thread, sew the end of a ribbon to the end of the other ribbon with a ¼″ seam allowance.

Tip

Sophie used ribbons that worked best in one direction. So if you're using ribbons that have a top and a bottom, make sure they're both pointed in the right direction. You wouldn't want the ice cream cones upside down on the belt!

4. With right sides facing out, carefully slide the ribbon around the webbing so the seam allowance is snug with the end of the webbing. Pin to secure the end. Continue pinning down the length of the webbing. Stop about 8″ from the end.

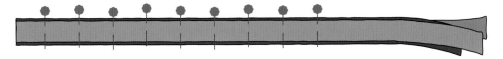

5. The raw edges of the ribbon will hang over the end of the webbing. Trim them ¼″ from the end of the webbing. Slip the webbing out from between the ribbons, and pin the ribbon ends together with right sides facing each other. Sew them together using a ¼″ seam allowance.

6. Pin the rest of the ribbon in place on the webbing. Both ribbons should be in the center of the webbing.

7. Fuse the front ribbon, pulling out the pins as you iron.

8. Turn the webbing over, and repeat the fusing on the other side. Allow the webbing to cool.

9. Using invisible thread and a zigzag stitch that is wide enough to catch the ribbons on both sides, slowly sew the ribbons to the webbing on each edge of the ribbon.

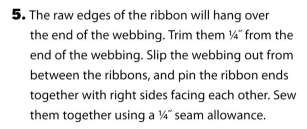

10. You now have a piece of webbing with ribbons on both sides. If the stitching didn't catch the ribbon in places, go back and add additional stitching now.

11. Slide 1 end of the webbing through both of the D-rings. Wrap the end back so there's a loop of webbing around the rings. Pin the end of the webbing to a side of the belt, allowing enough room that the rings can move a bit.

12. Using a jeans or leather needle, sew the loop closed, backtacking at the beginning and ending of the stitching.

embroidered pillowcase

It's really fun to embroider your name on a pillowcase. You can also design something totally unique to you or your family. Making the pillowcase is fast. The embroidery takes a little time, but you can do it anywhere—in the car or at a friend's, for example. Once you learn how to embroider, you may want to embroider other things, like a pair of jeans, a shirt, a scarf, or a towel. (Be sure to ask your parents if this is okay before you start!)

If you want to, you can make the pillowcase without the embroidery.

Finished size: 20″ × 28″

MATERIALS

- ☐ 1 piece of fabric 23″ × 40½″ for the main pillowcase

- ☐ 1 piece of fabric 1½″ × 40½″ for the accent strip

- ☐ 1 piece of white fabric 10″ × 40½″ for the pillowcase edge

- ☐ Matching thread

- ☐ Embroidery floss in a color that looks nice with the pillow fabrics (*optional*)

TOOLS AND SUPPLIES

- ☐ Sewing machine

- ☐ Iron

- ☐ Scissors or rotary cutter and mat

- ☐ Straight pins

- ☐ Embroidery needle (*optional*)

- ☐ Embroidery hoop (*optional*)

Sophie Says...

I liked making the pillowcase. It took longer than I expected, because the overlock stitch is slower than the regular straight stitch. My favorite part was embroidering my name. If you're embroidering on white fabric, be sure to trim the string from the knot underneath. Otherwise it shows through and looks like a stain. You can make this pillowcase for holidays like Halloween or Christmas. There are lots of holiday-themed prints available. For winter, make one out of something soft like flannel.

EMBROIDERING

If you want to embroider your name, do that first. See Embroidery (page 40) for general information.

1. On a computer, choose a fun font you like. Cursive fonts are easier to embroider because the letters flow together. You don't have to knot the embroidery floss when you're done with each letter.

2. Enlarge the font to about 2½″ high, and then type and print out your name. Tape the printout on a window with masking tape.

3. Fold the white edge fabric in half lengthwise. Then fold it in half again crosswise. Lightly press the folds to create creases to help you center your name. Place the fabric over the printout and tape it in place as shown in the diagram.

4. Using a chalk pencil or disappearing pen, trace your name onto the front of the fabric.

5. Place the fabric in an embroidery hoop.

6. Embroider the letters with the embroidery floss as shown (or use your favorite stitch).

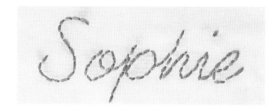

SEWING

1. After you've finished the embroidery, fold the white fabric in half lengthwise, wrong sides together. This covers up the back of the embroidery. Line up the edges and pin them. Press with an iron along the folded edge.

2. With right sides together, pin the long raw edges of the folded white fabric to the accent strip. Overlock or zigzag the edge of the white fabric to a side of the accent strip.

3. Press the overlocked seam toward the accent strip side of the seam.

4. With right sides together, pin the main fabric to the other side of the accent strip. Overlock or zigzag, and press.

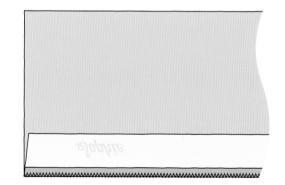

5. Fold the pillowcase in half with right sides together. Overlock or zigzag the 2 remaining sides, beginning with the white fabric.

6. Turn the pillowcase inside out. Poke the corners out with a chopstick if necessary to make them sharp and square.

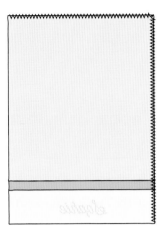

Sophie

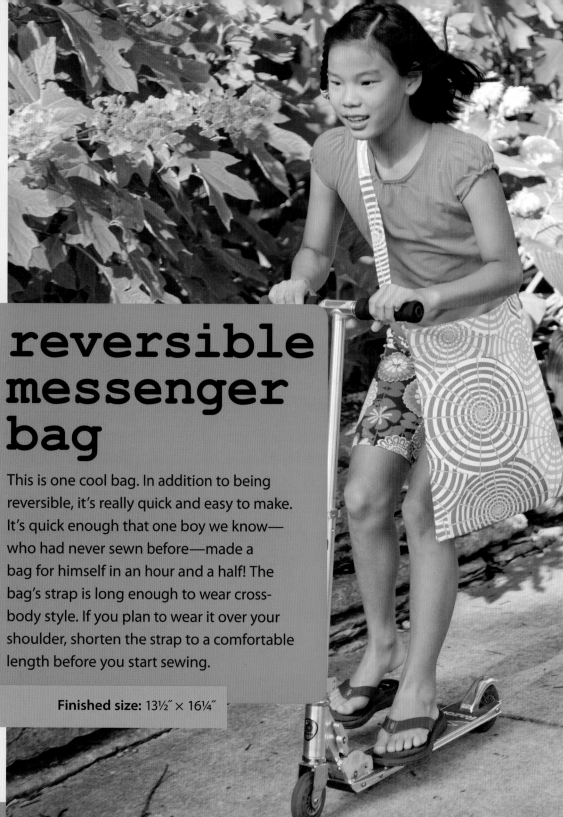

reversible messenger bag

This is one cool bag. In addition to being reversible, it's really quick and easy to make. It's quick enough that one boy we know— who had never sewn before—made a bag for himself in an hour and a half! The bag's strap is long enough to wear cross-body style. If you plan to wear it over your shoulder, shorten the strap to a comfortable length before you start sewing.

Finished size: 13½″ × 16¼″

MATERIALS

☐ ½ yard *each* of
2 different 40″-wide
or wider fabrics (see
Tip, at right)

☐ 45″ piece of yarn or string

☐ ½ yard of interfacing
(*optional*) (Refer to
Sophie Says, at right.)

☐ Matching thread

TOOLS AND SUPPLIES

☐ Sewing machine

☐ Iron

☐ Scissors or rotary cutter
and mat

☐ Universal sewing machine
needle

☐ Heavyweight jeans sewing
machine needle*

☐ Straight pins

☐ Binder clips (from an office
supply store)

** Sew with the universal needle until
the instructions say to switch.*

CUTTING

From each of
2 fabrics, cut:

☐ 1 strip 2½″ × 40″

☐ 1 piece 14″ × 33″

Sophie Says...

*This was one of my favorite projects because
it's reversible. That's pretty cool. I used leftover
fabric from the curtains in my room. Then I added
another favorite fabric. Upholstery-weight fabric was
heavy enough that I didn't need interfacing. If you choose
a lighter-weight fabric, use interfacing to make it a little
heavier.*

*One of my favorite things to sew was the strap. Turning it
inside out was a lot of fun. This is another project you could
do by yourself or with a friend after school. I made it in less
than an hour!*

Tip

*If you want the bag to be stronger and stiffer, use one fabric
that is a heavier weight, such as a home dec fabric, Cordura,
or cotton duck. The second can be regular quilting cotton.
It's fine to use quilting cotton for both fabrics, but the bag
will be much lighter weight and have less structure.*

SEWING
Make the strap

1. With the right sides of the 2 strips 2½″ × 40″ facing each
other, sew ¼″ from 1 long edge. Tie a knot at each end of
the yarn. Nestle it inside the 2 fabrics against the sewn
seam, with a knot hanging out on each end.

2. Sew across a short end of the strip (including the yarn or string). Then sew down the other long side, also ¼˝ from the edge. Be careful: Don't sew over the yarn as you sew the long side.

3. Pull gently on the yarn to turn the tube right side out. Press it flat. Then cut off the stitched end, releasing the yarn.

4. Topstitch the 2 long sides ⅛˝ from the edge. This will help keep the strap flat.

Assemble the bag

1. Place 1 of the 14˝ × 33˝ pieces face up. Pin the strap, with the matching fabric face *down* (see below), ¾˝ in from the side edges. Let 1½˝ hang over the short edges.

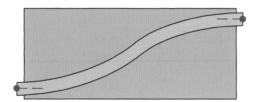

2. Place the second fabric face down, covering the strap. Pin the straps and the 2 large fabric pieces in place.

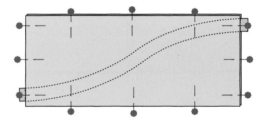

3. Starting in the middle of 1 long side, backtack and then sew around the edges of the bag ¼˝ from the edge. Stop 4˝ before your starting point, and backtack. This will leave a 4˝ gap.

4. Turn the bag right side out, pulling it through the 4″ gap. Push the corners out, and press the fabric sandwich flat, turning the edges of the gap to the inside of the bag.

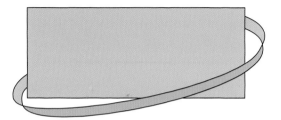

5. Fold the bag in half, aligning top and side edges. They'll be a bit too thick to pin easily, so use binder clips to hold them together. Switch to a jeans needle on your sewing machine. Then topstitch down both sides to close them. Make sure to backtack at the top and bottom to reinforce the seams. You can now use the bag with either side facing out.

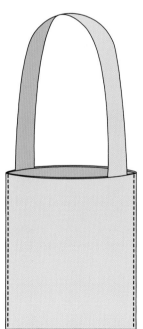

backpack decorations

Sophie says this is one of her favorite projects in the book. She had a really good time making these decorations with her friends. You can get creative making the stacked flowers and ice cream cones from felted wool. You can use beads, embroidery, or even sequins. Just make sure that you stitch them on carefully so they don't fall off!

Finished size: Varies

MATERIALS

For stacked flower:

- ☐ Felted wool in assorted colors
- ☐ Felted wool strap or piece of thin ribbon 2″ long and narrow enough to fit through the opening of the backpack clip
- ☐ Matching thread
- ☐ Embroidery floss
- ☐ Backpack clip (can be found in the notions or purse-making section of a fabric store)
- ☐ Stuffing
- ☐ Sequins or beads (*optional*)

For ice cream cone:

- ☐ Felted wool in assorted colors
- ☐ Felted wool strap or piece of thin ribbon 2″ long and narrow enough to fit through the opening of the backpack clip
- ☐ Matching thread
- ☐ Embroidery floss
- ☐ Backpack clip
- ☐ Stuffing
- ☐ Sequins or beads (*optional*)

TOOLS AND SUPPLIES

- ☐ Scissors
- ☐ Straight pins
- ☐ Hand-sewing needle
- ☐ Embroidery needle

Sophie Says...

This project is very fun and interesting because of all of the choices. I liked all of the different funky flowers and shapes.
You can add beads and even embroider your name. All of the different colors and designs make your keychain colorful.

You have to really be careful about cutting out the wool with the patterns. It's important to trace them carefully. Cut them slowly with sharp scissors, or your project might look sloppy.

You could make these decorations as pincushions or as pins to wear. We made them for backpacks. It would be a fun activity at a birthday party. We had seven girls all working on them at the same time. It was really fun!

SEWING
Stacked flower

Patterns are on pages 92 and 93.

1. Trace the patterns onto the felt of your choice. Cut them out.

2. Arrange the cut pieces the way you like them on top of a circle or square of felt. Use sequins or beads for the centers of the flowers. Sew with thread and needle. You can even embroider designs on the felt if you want.

3. If you use the long-petaled flower, you can tuck the ends under in the middle to make loops for petals. Sew the ends in place.

4. Once the flower is complete, trace the outline of the outside edge onto a piece of felt to make the backing. Cut out the backing.

5. With wrong sides together, hand sew the backing to the front around the outside edge, using either a blanket stitch or a running stitch (see Embroidery, page 40). Leave a 1″ gap at the top.

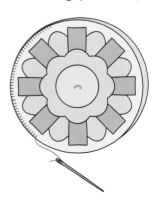

6. Insert stuffing between the layers of felt, using a pencil or chopstick.

7. Thread the felt strip through the opening of the backpack clip and fold over.

8. Insert the ends of the strip into the gap and stitch closed.

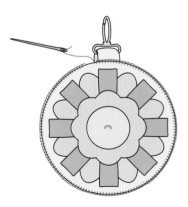

Try your own flower variations!

Ice cream cone

Patterns are on pages 92 and 93.

1. Trace the patterns onto the felt of your choice. Cut them out.

2. Arrange as desired. You can sew sequins or beads for sprinkles or decorations on the ice cream or the cone. This will also help secure the ice cream scoops to the cone base.

3. Once the ice cream cone is complete, trace the outline of it onto a piece of felt to make the backing. Cut out the backing.

4. With wrong sides together, hand sew the backing to the front around the outside edge, using either a blanket stitch or a running stitch (see Embroidery, page 40). Leave a 1˝ gap at the top.

5. Using a pencil or chopstick, insert stuffing between the layers of felt.

6. Thread the felt strip through the opening of the backpack clip. Insert the ends into the gap on the decoration, and stitch it closed.

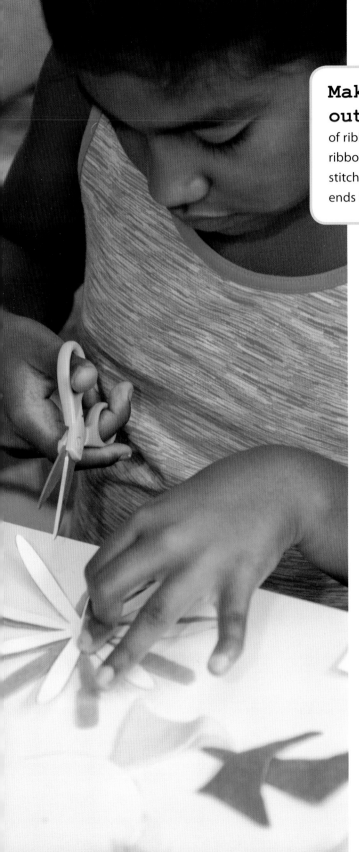

Make your own design out of scraps. If you use 8″ of ribbon instead of a backpack clip, fold the ribbon in half, insert the fold into the gap, and stitch it closed. You can use the loose ribbon ends to tie the decoration on.

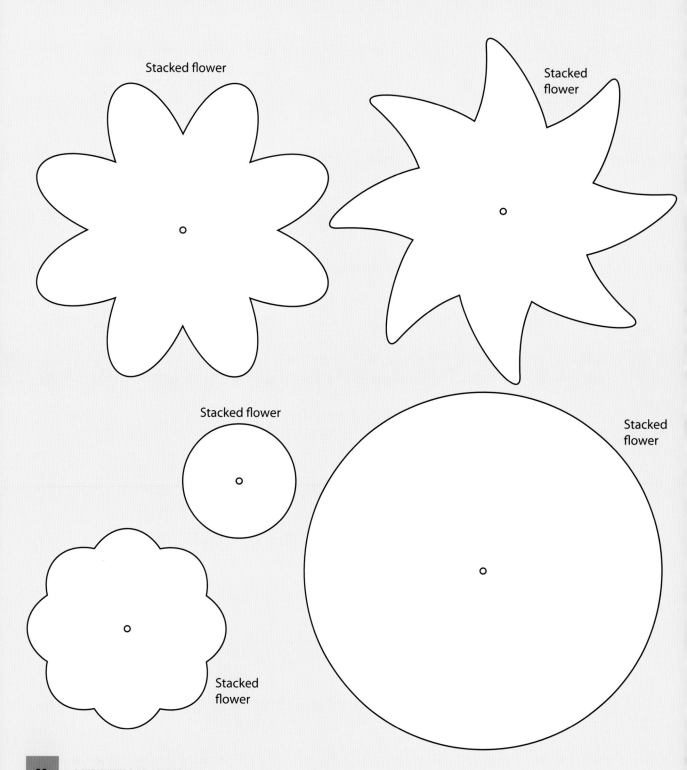

Stacked flower

Stacked flower

Stacked flower

Stacked flower

Stacked flower

Stacked flower

A KID'S GUIDE TO SEWING

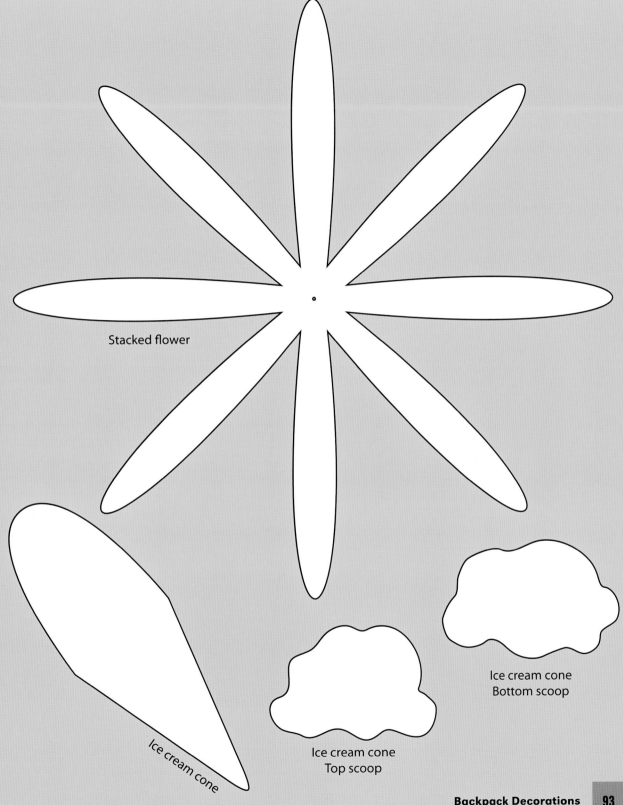

Stacked flower

Ice cream cone

Ice cream cone
Top scoop

Ice cream cone
Bottom scoop

quilted place mats

It's a lot more fun to set the table when you've made the place mats! These quilted place mats are easy to make, and you can throw them in the wash if you spill spaghetti sauce on them. We're showing you an easy version, plus a more advanced one that is like a miniature crazy quilt. A crazy quilt is made from scraps. It takes longer to make, because you have so many pieces to sew together. For both place mats, you get to learn how to do patchwork and simple quilting. The nice thing about place mats is that they don't all have to match. So you can do some that are easy, and others that are more challenging.

Finished size: 16½″ × 13″

simple or "crazy"

MATERIALS

For simple place mat:

- ¼ yard cotton print fabric for the top and bottom strips (we used green)

- Assorted cotton fabric pieces for the center strip (we used yellow)

- ½ yard cotton fabric for backing

- 13¼″ × 16¾″ piece of cotton batting

- Matching thread

For "crazy" (advanced) place mat:

- Assorted cotton quilting-weight fabrics totaling ½ yard

- ½ yard cotton fabric for backing

- 13¼″ × 16¾″ piece of cotton batting

- Matching thread

TOOLS AND SUPPLIES

- Sewing machine

- Scissors or rotary cutter and mat

- Straight pins

Simple place mat

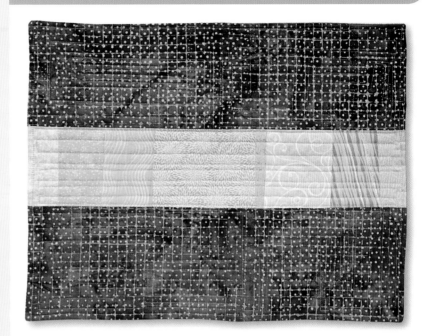

CUT THE FABRIC

1. From the green fabric, cut 2 strips 5¼″ × 17″.

2. From the yellow fabric, cut a variety of 4″-high strips of different widths to equal 17″ once sewn together. (It's easiest to make it a bit longer and then trim it down to 17″.)

For example: You could cut 2 pieces 1″ wide, 3 pieces 2″ wide, 3 pieces 3″ wide, and 1 piece 5″ wide.

You don't need to be exact. As long as they're all 4″ high, you can cut them any width you want. Look at the photo (above) and the drawing (page 96) to see how they will look. If you like calculating exactly what width strips to cut, don't forget that the seam allowance means the finished strips will each be ½″ narrower than the size you cut.

3. From the backing fabric, cut 1 piece 13½″ × 17″. Set it aside.

PIECE THE TOP *Use a ¼″ seam allowance for this project.*

1. Sew the yellow strips together along their 4″-long sides to make a row. Press the seams open with an iron. Check to see that the row is at least 17″ long before you go any further. If it is longer, trim it down to 17″.

2. Pin a green strip to an edge of the yellow row, right sides together, and sew. Press the seam open with an iron.

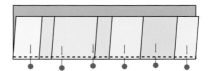

3. Pin the remaining strip to the other edge of the yellow row, right sides together, and sew. Press the seam open with an iron.

ASSEMBLE THE LAYERS

1. With right sides together, stack the backing and pieced place mat top. Center the batting on top of this stack. It's a bit smaller than the top and bottom, so it'll be about ⅛″ away from the edges. Smooth from the center to the edges to make sure there are no wrinkles in any of the layers. Pin the stack together in several places to keep it from slipping.

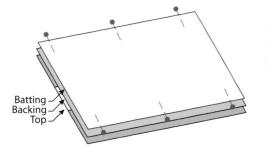

2. Stitch ¼″ away from the edge on 3 sides.

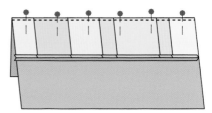

3. With scissors, carefully trim the batting ¼″ from the open side, making sure not to cut the fabric. Trim the corners off close to the stitching. This will make the corners less bulky.

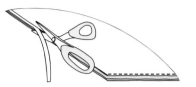

4. Turn the place mat right side out. Use a chopstick to poke the corners out and make them neat. Carefully tuck and then fold in the raw edges ¼″ over the edge of the batting.

5. Topstitch the end closed, and continue topstitching all the way around the piece. Sew as close to the edge as you can while still being able to sew a straight line. Use the edge of the presser foot as a guide to keep an even seam.

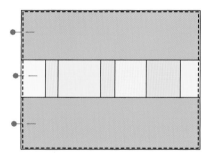

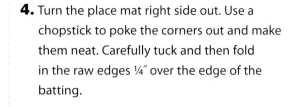

Sophie's quilting tips

To quilt in straight lines, put masking tape on the fabric and sew next to it. I lined the tape up by using a triangle and a ruler. Be careful not to sew onto the masking tape or you might have a hard time taking it off. (If you do, you can use tweezers or your fingernails to pull out the little bits of tape.) Also, be sure to remove the masking tape the same day. If you don't, the tape may leave sticky stuff behind. I would use the same color thread as the fabric in the place mat. If you use a thread that's a different color, it will be more obvious if you make a mistake. If you use a thread that blends into the fabric, your mistakes won't show as much.

Quilting

Quilting is the stitching that goes through all three layers to hold them together. You can quilt in straight lines, at angles, in waves, or in any pattern you choose. Just make sure that there's no area bigger than 1″ × 1″ that doesn't have stitching to keep the batting in place. Quilt with the top of the place mat facing up using a thread color that looks good with the top. If you have a walking foot, you'll find it helpful in quilting this project.

"Crazy" (advanced) place mat

Sophie Says...

This is, for sure, a crazy, colorful miniature quilt that you can use for a place mat. There are so many different shapes and sizes of pieces that every place mat you make will be unique. You can use scraps or any fabrics of your choice. A fun idea is to make a place mat for each member of the family in his or her favorite color.

CRAZY PIECE THE TOP

To make the top of the place mat, use a technique called crazy piecing, in which no two pieces are the same. You sew pieces to each other pretty randomly. Once the pieced top is large enough, you trim it down to size. Crazy piecing is especially fun if you like to make things up as you go.

Sophie's pink place mat is fairly detailed. It has nearly 70 pieces made out of scraps from about 20 different fabrics. If you like the idea of crazy piecing but want to keep it simpler, just use larger pieces.

Sew fabrics together into irregular units and trim them down. Then sew those units together. Sew along straight lines and avoid sewing into corners.

1. Cut 2 irregular pieces with sides measuring 2″–5″ long. Use larger pieces for a simpler top, or smaller pieces for a more complex top.

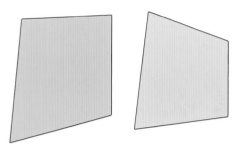

2. Align the edges of the 2 pieces with right sides together, and sew ¼″ from the edge. Press the seam open with an iron.

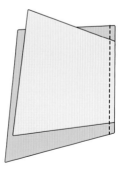

3. Trim an edge so the unit has 1 straight side.

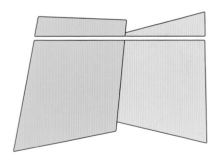

4. Repeat Steps 1–3 to make other pieced pairs.

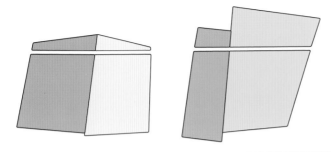

5. Align 2 pieced pairs, with right sides facing, along their straight edges. Sew, and then press the seam open.

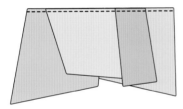

6. Trim this new unit so it's straight on 1 side.

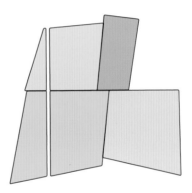

7. Repeat the previous steps to build up and sew together different-sized units. You can also sew long strips to the side of some units.

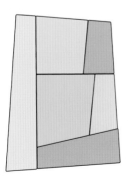

8. Once your pieced top is larger than the 13½″ × 17″ backing piece, trim it to 13½″ × 17″.

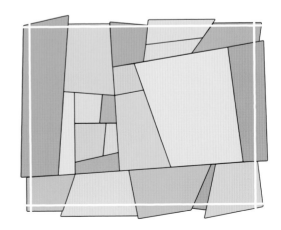

ASSEMBLE THE LAYERS AND QUILT IT

From the backing fabric, cut 1 piece 13½˝ × 17˝.

Follow the steps in Assemble the Layers for *Simple Place Mat* (pages 96 and 97) to assemble, stitch, and quilt the place mat.

pool cover-up

It's hard to find cute pool cover-ups for tweens and teens, so why not make your own? You can make it with or without straps. The secret to this project is learning how to use elastic thread. Once you've figured it out, you'll realize that you can use the same pattern for making sundresses or summer shirts. All you have to do is change the fabric and the length. You can make this cover-up in cotton, or in stretchy French terry cloth for an absorbent version.

MATERIALS

- ☐ Cotton fabric or stretch terry cloth at least 52″ wide (To determine the amount of fabric needed, refer to Make the Main Piece, Step 1, below right. You will need to add a bit of extra fabric—⅛ yard or so—for the straps.)

- ☐ 24″ piece of sturdy string or cord

- ☐ Elastic thread

- ☐ Matching thread

TOOLS AND SUPPLIES

- ☐ Sewing machine

- ☐ Scissors or rotary cutter and mat

- ☐ Measuring tape

- ☐ Iron

- ☐ Straight pins

Sophie Says...

I really enjoyed using the elastic thread to make the smocking on the top. It was fun to watch the fabric go from being flat to being bumpy and smocked. You could even use this idea to make a skirt to wear to the pool or to the beach. I'd practice using the elastic thread. Find a piece of cloth that's the same width as the one you plan to sew. After you've done the smocking, try it on. See if it's going to fit. Make it wider or smaller if it doesn't. Depending on the brand of thread and your sewing machine, the amount of stretch in the smocking might be different.

SEWING
Make the main piece

1. Measure around the widest part of your bust and hips. Take the larger of these 2 measurements and double it. This is the cut width for the fabric. Measure from your armpit to the level where you want the hem to fall. Add 2″. This is the cut length for the fabric. Cut the fabric to size. (For help on measuring, see Measuring Your Body, page 42.)

2. Overlock or zigzag the fabric's long edges to keep them from raveling.

3. Fold the fabric in half lengthwise with the right sides together. Overlock or zigzag the side seam together along the cut edges. Now you have a tube.

4. Fold the top edge of the tube over to the wrong side of the fabric by 1˝. Press, pin, and zigzag the hem.

5. Repeat Step 4 for the bottom edge. You should now have a large rectangular tube of fabric with finished edges.

Create the smocking

Tip

If you wish, you can buy presmocked fabric to make the job easier. If you use the elastic thread, check the tension of your smocking stitches on a test piece of fabric first and adjust it as necessary (see Sophie Says, page 103).

1. Wind the elastic thread *by hand* onto a bobbin. Wind it loosely without stretching the thread. Do not use the machine's bobbin-winding mechanism to do this! It is important to take the time to wind it by hand.

2. Load the bobbin into the sewing machine, but keep the top of the machine threaded with regular thread. Pull long tails of both threads through before you start sewing. Change the stitch length to the longest setting.

3. With the right side of the tube facing up, line up the presser foot along the top hem at the side seam.

4. Backtack for about 1″. Then sew a line of straight stitches, parallel to the top hem, around the entire fabric tube. When you reach the starting point again, backtack. Leave a long tail of both threads, and cut the threads.

5. Repeat this with another row of stitches parallel to the first row, and continue in this manner until the smocked section is as long as you want it to be. Use the presser foot as a guide for spacing the rows of stitches. Smooth the fabric out if it starts to bunch up, and be careful not to sew over the long thread tails you left from the previous rows.

6. Take the long elastic tails at the beginning and end of each row of stitches, and tie them together securely with 3 or 4 knots. This holds the rows of smocking stitches in place. Trim the thread tails.

7. Gently press the smocked section with the steam setting of the iron, and it should gather up evenly.

Make the straps

If you want to add straps, just stitch some seamed strips of fabric to the inside of the front top edge. You could stitch them in place at the back, too, or leave the straps loose to tie behind your neck halter style.

Terry cloth knits stretch a lot in one direction and only a little in the other. For straps, cut the terry cloth strips in the direction that does not stretch much.

1. Cut the terry cloth into 2 strips 1½″ × 20″. Cut a 24″ piece of sturdy string or cord. Knot both ends.

2. With the right side of a strip facing up, lay the cord in the middle of the strip. Have both ends of the cord hanging beyond the ends of the strip. Fold the strip with its right sides together. Sew across a narrow end. Then sew down the long raw edges, ¼″ from the edge. Make sure the cord does not get caught in the long seam.

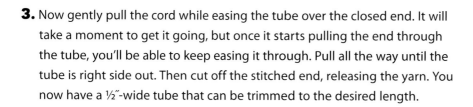

3. Now gently pull the cord while easing the tube over the closed end. It will take a moment to get it going, but once it starts pulling the end through the tube, you'll be able to keep easing it through. Pull all the way until the tube is right side out. Then cut off the stitched end, releasing the yarn. You now have a ½″-wide tube that can be trimmed to the desired length.

4. Repeat Steps 2 and 3 with the second strip.

5. Try on the cover-up and pin the straps where they are comfortable. Pin the ends of the straps to the inside right at the top row of smocking. Take off the cover-up (be careful of the pins) and sew the tube ends inside the top. As you stitch the straps to the cover-up, be sure not to stitch through the elastic thread because that would weaken the thread. Trim the excess length of the straps.

gini's tiered skirt

Our friend Gini has been making versions of this skirt for Sophie since Sophie was in first grade. Gini, who is a retired teacher, generously shared her tips for making these skirts so other girls could make them on their own. You can make a simple skirt with two tiers. Or you can make one with more tiers. Gini and Sophie both love super bright prints all mixed together. Which combination of fabrics would you use?

MATERIALS

Read Measuring and Skirt Calculations (at right) to figure out how much fabric and elastic you need.

☐ Fabric for the skirt top tier

☐ Fabric for the skirt bottom tier

☐ 1 package of extra-wide ½˝ double-fold binding tape *or* ¼ yard fabric to make your own binding using the project instructions

☐ ¾˝-wide elastic

☐ Matching thread

TOOLS AND SUPPLIES

☐ Sewing machine

☐ Scissors or rotary cutter and mat

☐ Iron

☐ Straight pins

☐ Thread

☐ Chalk or water-soluble marking pen

Sophie Says...

I learned a lot making the skirt! All the colors are fun to choose, too. It took me about 2½ hours from start to finish. My favorite part was gathering the fabric to make the ruffle. If you want a fuller skirt with more gathers, you can make the base piece longer so you will have more gathering at the seam. You can make this project with seasonal, novelty, or holiday fabric also.

Measuring and Skirt Calculations

The most important thing about making clothes is to make them comfortable. To be sure your skirt will fit just right, you'll need to measure yourself and do some simple math. It's best to use a fabric measuring tape so you can wrap it around your body to get accurate measurements. Once you've taken each measurement, write it in the worksheet so you have all of the measurements in one place. For help on measuring, see Measuring Your Body (page 42).

Use the worksheet on page 110 to calculate your measurements!

CUTTING

Use your measurements and skirt calculations to determine the size of the pieces needed. Cut the top tier and the bottom tier. Cut the elastic the size of your waist. Here are sample measurements for an average size 12:

☐ Cut a piece of fabric 7˝ × 36˝ for skirt top tier.

☐ Cut a piece of fabric 14˝ × 40˝ for skirt bottom tier.

☐ Cut a 45˝ piece of binding tape.

☐ Cut 26˝ of ¾˝-wide elastic.

1. *Measure your waist right at your belly button:* _____ *inches*

2. *Measure your hips at the widest point:* _____ *inches*

3. *Measure the length from your waist to your knee:* _____ *inches*

If your hip measurement is <u>smaller than 38˝</u>:

TOP TIER OF SKIRT: *Cut a piece of fabric 7˝ high from selvage to selvage if using a 42˝-wide fabric (or less than selvage to selvage if you want a trimmer fit).*

BOTTOM TIER OF SKIRT: *Subtract 7½˝ from your waist-to-knee measurement. This is the length to cut the fabric. Cut the width from selvage to selvage.*

If your waist or hip measurement is <u>larger than 38˝</u>:

If your hips or waist measure more than 38˝ and you want to use fabric that's 42˝ from selvage to selvage, you will need to piece together the tiers. Here's how to figure out the measurements:

CUT FOR TOP TIER OF SKIRT: *7˝ high × (hip measurement + 2˝) wide, piecing together 7˝-high strips if necessary to make it wide enough*

CUT FOR BOTTOM TIER OF SKIRT: *(Length from waist to knee − 7½˝) high × width used for top tier (or greater if you want a fuller fit)*

To make a skirt with multiple tiers or a longer skirt (measure from waist to desired hem length):

FOR WIDTH OF TIERS: *Use the formulas above.*

FOR LENGTH OF TIERS:

1. *Measurement from waist to hem ÷ number of tiers = finished width of each tier*

2. *Then calculate the cut width of each tier:*

Top tier = *finished width + 1¾˝ (for channel and seam allowance)*

Remaining tiers = *finished width + ½˝ (for seam allowances at top and bottom)*

For example:

If the measurement from waist to hem is 22˝ and you want a skirt with 4 tiers, the formula would be 22˝ ÷ 4 = 5½˝. Then you need to add the channel and seam allowances to that width. So you get:

Top tier: 5½˝ + 1¾˝ (for channel and seam allowance) = 7¼˝ cut width

Remaining tiers: 5½˝ + ½˝ (for seam allowances) = 6˝ cut width

SEWING *This project uses a ¼″ seam allowance.*

Make the skirt

1. To make a channel for the elastic, fold the top of the top tier down ¼″. Press.

2. Then fold the top tier down another 1¼″. (Note: Make sure you fold it at least ⅜″ larger than the width of the elastic you're using. Measure the actual width of the elastic, because ¾″ elastic is sometimes wider than ¾″.) Press, and set aside.

3. Using the longest stitch your machine can make, stitch ¼″ from the top of the bottom tier, leaving long thread tails at each end. This is called a "basting stitch."

4. Pull the ends of the thread on the bottom tier gently and slide the fabric a little bit to begin gathering up the ruffle.

5. Lay the top tier next to the bottom tier. If you have cut the bottom tier wider than the top tier, you need to make them the same width by gathering the bottom tier. Try to distribute the fabric evenly in the bottom tier so it's not all bunched together.

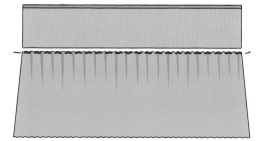

6. With right sides facing and raw edges aligned, pin the tiers together. Using a ¼″ seam allowance and an overlock or zigzag stitch, sew the tiers together.

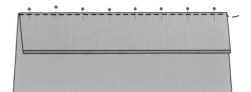

7. Pin the sides together, opening up the pressed channel for the elastic at the top of the skirt. Using a ¼″ seam allowance and an overlock or zigzag stitch, sew the sides together.

8. Refold the channel at the top. Use a zigzag stitch to topstitch along the inside folded edge. Make sure to catch the edge with each stitch. Leave a 3″-long gap at the side seam so you'll be able to get the elastic in.

9. Attach a safety pin to 1 end of the elastic. Push the elastic through the channel. Make sure not to twist it as you go.

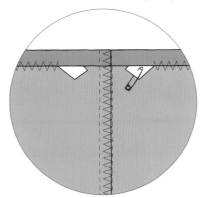

10. Sew the ends of the elastic together with a zigzag stitch, backtacking at each end.

11. Insert the elastic back into the channel and topstitch the gap closed.

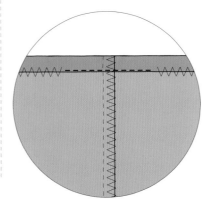

Bind the bottom skirt edge

This skirt has a fabric binding around the bottom that makes it look super neat. If you are using prepackaged binding, skip to Step 5.

1. Cut 2 strips 2″ × width of fabric (selvage to selvage). With right sides together and using a ¼″ seam allowance, sew the ends of the strips together. This makes a long strip. Press the seam of the strip open.

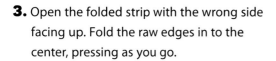

2. With the right sides facing out, fold the long strip in half lengthwise, pressing as you go.

3. Open the folded strip with the wrong side facing up. Fold the raw edges in to the center, pressing as you go.

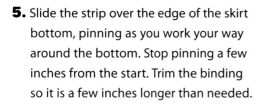

4. Fold the strip in half again along the original center crease, so you have a strip with no raw edges showing. Press it flat.

5. Slide the strip over the edge of the skirt bottom, pinning as you work your way around the bottom. Stop pinning a few inches from the start. Trim the binding so it is a few inches longer than needed.

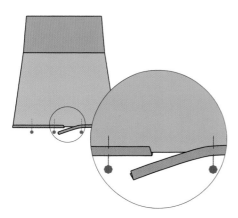

6. With chalk, mark a point 3″ from the beginning of the binding strip. Beginning at the chalked point, topstitch the binding strip onto the hem of the skirt about ⅛″ from the edge. Be sure the stitching is catching the folded edge of the binding on both the front and the back.

7. Stop stitching about 3″ before you reach the loose piece of binding where you started. Trim the strip ends so they overlap by ½″.

8. With right sides together, unfold the strip and pin the starting end to the tail end. Using a ¼″ seam allowance, sew the ends together.

9. Using your fingers, refold the strip and wrap it around the remaining part of the skirt. Pin the closed binding in place, and finish top-stitching the hem.

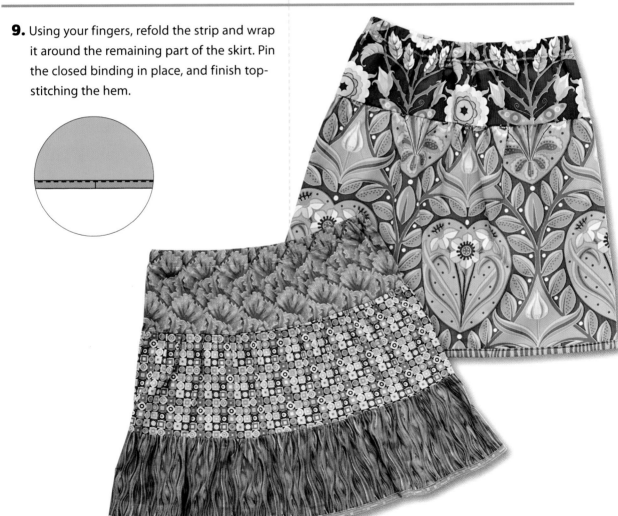

insulated lunch bag

Finished size: 7½″ wide × 14½″ high × 5″ deep

Lunch is so much more fun when you have a bag that you like, made in just the right size. This is a great project for both boys and girls. Search the quilting cotton section of a chain store or your local quilt shop to find fabric in your favorite color or print. You could even use fabric with the logo of your favorite team. You can laminate the fabric yourself with special iron-on plastic to make it water resistant. Don't forget to get the lining and insulation fabrics at the same time, if you want your favorite foods to stay cold!

MATERIALS

- ½ yard of quilting-weight cotton fabric for outside

- ½ yard of nylon lining fabric for inside (we used ripstop nylon but other fabrics will work)

- ½ yard of insulated lining or interfacing (such as Insul-Fleece)

- 1 yard of 15″-wide iron-on laminating plastic (also called iron-on vinyl)

- Matching thread

- Elastic ponytail holder (for the closure)

- 1″ button

TOOLS AND SUPPLIES

- Sewing machine

- Iron

- Straight pins

- Binder clips (from office supply store)

- Hand-sewing needle

- Thread

Sophie Says...

This project is medium in difficulty. There are a lot of layers to sew through. Some of the sewing is a little awkward. It looks really good, though, when it's finished. One of the exciting parts for me was laminating the fabric. You just iron on this magical stuff. Then your regular cotton fabric becomes laminated! Laminating the fabric makes it easier to clean and keeps it from getting wet.

I use a lunch bag every day at school and at summer camp. It's fun to have a lunch bag that I can make and customize. For example, you could have lunch bags for holidays. I want to look for some spooky jack-o'-lantern fabric. Then I can laminate it to make a fun Halloween lunch bag. You can even change the size of the bag to fit what you carry in your lunch.

LAMINATE THE FABRIC

1. Cut a piece of the cotton fabric 15″ × 36″.

2. Follow the directions that came with the laminating plastic to iron it onto the cotton fabric. In general, peel the wax paper backing off the plastic, but keep the backing. Then line up the plastic, with the sticky side down, on the right side of the fabric. Place the wax paper backing on top of the plastic. Then sandwich all 3 layers (cotton fabric, plastic, and wax paper) between 2 pressing cloths, a cloth on the top and another on the bottom. Finally, iron all the layers. It is really important to *fully cover* your project with a pressing cloth so that no parts of the plastic melt on your iron or ironing board. Melted plastic makes a big mess and can ruin your ironing board cover and your iron.

CUTTING

From laminated fabric, cut:

- ☐ 2 front and back panels 8″ × 15″
- ☐ 2 side panels 6″ × 15″
- ☐ 1 bottom panel 6″ × 8″

From lining fabric, cut:

- ☐ 2 front and back panels 8″ × 15″
- ☐ 2 side panels 6″ × 15″
- ☐ 1 bottom panel 6″ × 8″

From insulated lining, cut:

- ☐ 2 front and back pieces 7½″ × 9¾″
- ☐ 2 side panels 5½″ × 9¾″
- ☐ 1 bottom panel 5½″ × 7½″

SEWING

Make side and bottom panels

1. Place the front panel fabric right side down. Center the insulation ¼″ from the bottom edge and ¼″ from the sides. Using a thread that looks nice on the cotton fabric (because you'll see the thread), sew across the top edge of the insulation. This holds it in place.

2. With right sides facing each other, place the front panel (from Step 1) on the front panel lining. Fasten them together with binder clips. Use these instead of pins, because pins leave holes in the laminated fabric.

3. Sew the lining and laminated fabric together along the sides and top, ¼″ from the edges. Leave the bottom open.

4. Turn assembled panel right side out. Poke the corners out from the inside with a capped ballpoint pen or a chopstick.

5. Fold the open edges ¼˝ in at the bottom. Topstitch closed.

6. The laminated fabric might be wrinkled from being turned inside out. You can put it back under the pressing cloth, cover it *fully* with the wax paper, and press it again. It's amazing how well this simple touching up works.

7. Repeat Steps 1–6 for the back and 2 side panels, using the back and side pieces.

8. For the bottom panel, center the insulation on the cotton fabric, leaving ¼˝ around all 4 sides. Then follow Steps 2–6.

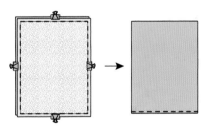

9. Make a small mark centered 3˝ from the top of the back panel. This is where you'll attach the ponytail holder. Securely hand stitch or machine zigzag the ponytail holder to the bag.

10. Make a small mark centered 6˝ from the top of the front panel. This is where you'll attach the button. Sew the button to the bag.

Join side and bottom panels

Topstitching makes it easier to sew the panels together.

1. With lining sides together, sew the back panel to the bottom panel ⅛″ from the edge. You might be carrying fairly heavy things in this bag, so make the seams stronger by backtacking at the beginning and end of the stitching.

2. Repeat Step 1 using the side panels and front panel.

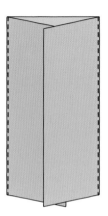

3. With lining sides together, sew the long edges of the side panels (from Step 2) to the long edges of the back panel (from Step 1). Then sew the bottom panel to the bottom edges of the sides and front to create the bag shape.

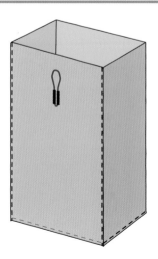

cuddle fleece patchwork throw

This project is not super complicated. But because it's big, it takes a while to finish. As you work on it, you will learn the basics of making a quilt—sewing patchwork, quilting, and binding. You can even use the same techniques on a smaller scale to sew a striped place mat. It's a fun project to do with a friend, because you can talk while you work. If you set up your sewing table so someone can sit across from you, your friend will be able to "catch" the weight of the quilt, making it easier to sew. The pinning takes time, but it's the same technique over and over again. So you could listen to music while you sew. We give you two versions here—one simple and one a bit more challenging. Take your pick!

Finished size: approximately 44˝ × 82˝

simple
or fancy

MATERIALS

For simple throw:

- ☐ 2¾ yards of white quilting cotton for the pieced top
- ☐ 1½ yards *each* of 3 different blue quilting cottons for the pieced top
- ☐ 2½ yards of 56″-wide cuddle fleece for the backing
- ☐ 1⅛ yards of blue quilting fabric for the binding
- ☐ Matching thread

For fancy multicolored throw:

- ☐ 1½ yards of solid purple quilting cotton for the strips
- ☐ 3 yards total of assorted multicolored prints for the pieced strips
- ☐ 2½ yards of 56″-wide cuddle fleece for the backing
- ☐ 1⅛ yards of deep purple quilting cotton for the binding
- ☐ Matching thread

TOOLS AND SUPPLIES

- ☐ Sewing machine
- ☐ Scissors or rotary cutter and mat
- ☐ Straight pins
- ☐ Metal bicycle pants clips (*optional*) or large safety pins
- ☐ Walking foot for quilting (*optional*)

Sophie Says...

This throw is soft and warm. I like curling up with it while reading or watching movies. There are two versions. The blue-and-white one is simpler and faster to make. You just use one fabric per strip. The multicolored version is harder and takes more time. You have to piece fabrics together to make the strips for that one. I wanted to make one that was really colorful. So I enjoyed choosing all of the patterns and colors for the multicolored version.

This project is harder than others to sew because it's so big. If you want to make it a little bit easier, you can use bicycle clips. They keep the sides rolled neatly while you sew. Ask a friend or family member to help you keep it straight when you are pinning and sewing.

Simple throw

Cutting lengthwise means the long way, with the fabric grain.

CUTTING

From white fabric for top, cut lengthwise:

☐ 20 strips 2½″ × 48″

From *each* of the 3 blue fabrics for top, cut lengthwise:

☐ 7 strips 2½″ × 48″

From blue binding fabric, cut:

☐ 7 pieces 5″ × 40″

From cuddle fleece, cut:

☐ 1 piece 48″ × 84″

Tip

Cuddle fleece sheds when you cut it. As soon as you cut it to size, overlock or zigzag the edges to help control the shedding. Vacuum to help keep the fuzzies from getting everywhere!

SEW THE THROW

Use a ¼″ seam allowance for this project.

1. Spread the fleece backing on the floor with the softer side facing down. Fleece stretches easily, so try to keep it in a rectangular shape. Carefully smooth a 2½″ × 48″ blue cotton strip, right side up, across the top. Line up 1 end flush with 1 edge of the fleece. Pin it in place. *This is the only strip that you will attach with its right side facing up. The rest you will pin and sew on wrong side up. Then you'll flip them to be right side up and add the next strip. The photos below show you how this works, using the fancy multicolored version as an example.*

2. Roll up all but about 10″ of the fleece, leaving the pinned strip exposed. Using bicycle clips or large safety pins, clip the fleece so it doesn't unroll. Sew the first strip to the fleece ¼″ from the edge, leaving the pins in place.

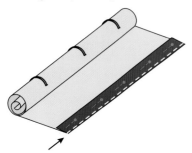

Tip

If the long roll of fleece is a bit tricky to sew by yourself, set up a chair on the other side of the table from the sewing machine. Have a friend help you guide it through as you sew.

3. Take off the clip and unroll the throw a few inches. Reclip it in place. Smooth a white strip, face down, directly on top of the blue strip. Match 1 edge of the white strip to the unsewn edge of the blue strip, and pin it in place through all the layers. Sew the strips to the fleece backing ¼″ from the pinned edge.

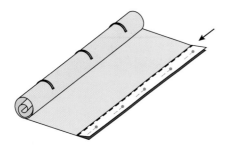

4. Unroll the throw further, and clip it in place. Remove the pins from the strip you just sewed. Flip the top strip over so the right side is facing up. Smooth it flat against the fleece. Carefully place a strip of the second blue fabric face down on the white strip you just flipped over. Pin the new strip in place.

5. Once again, you'll sew the strips to the backing ¼″ from their edges. But this time, sew across starting from the opposite side. Alternating sides helps keep the throw from getting out of shape.

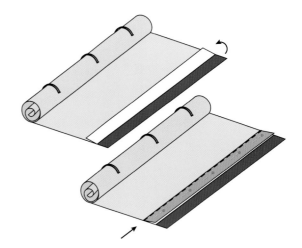

6. Repeat Steps 3–5, alternating white and blue strips in the following sequence: white, blue 1, white, blue 2, white, blue 3, and then back to white, blue 1, and so on. Remember to sew from the opposite edge of the throw with each new strip. The strip ends probably won't line up exactly, but don't worry. They are extra long and you'll trim them later.

7. Once you've sewn the last strip on, flip it over and sew its final edge flat to the backing. There will be extra fleece after the last strip.

8. Trim the length of the fleece even with the edge of the final strip.

9. Spread the throw out fully on the floor. Using a yardstick and chalk, mark a straight line along each edge of the quilt. Trim it even.

BIND THE THROW

1. Sew the 5″ binding strips together, end to end with right sides together, using a ¼″ seam. This will make 1 long strip. Press the seams open.

2. Fold and press the long strip in half lengthwise. Open the strip back up and press both sides in to the center.

3. Fold in half again, and press.

4. Measure the length of the throw. Then cut 2 binding strips, each 1″ longer than this measurement.

5. Fold in the strips' cut ends ½″, and press.

6. Tuck a long side edge of the throw into the folded binding. Make sure it fits snugly, and keep the back and front of the binding lined up with each other. Pin it in place.

7. Topstitch the binding to the throw ⅛″–¼″ from the inside edge of the binding. Backtack at the beginning and end of the stitching. The stitching will go through all the layers—the top of the binding, the throw, and the bottom of the binding.

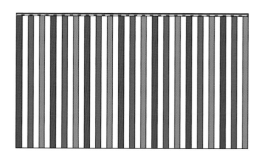

8. Repeat Steps 6 and 7 for the other long side.

9. Measure the width of the throw. Cut 2 binding strips, each 1″ longer than this measurement. Repeat Steps 5–7 to bind the 2 ends of the throw.

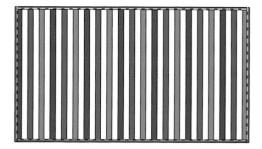

Fancy multicolored throw

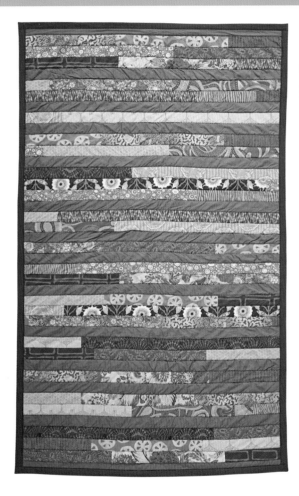

CUTTING

> Cutting lengthwise means the long way, with the fabric grain.

From solid purple fabric for top, cut lengthwise:

☐ 14 strips 2½" × 48"

From assorted multicolored prints, cut crosswise:

☐ 30 to 35 strips 2½" × 40" (Cut these strips into pieces of varying lengths. Cut none of them shorter than 6".)

From cuddle fleece, cut:

☐ 1 piece 48" × 84"

From deep purple binding fabric, cut:

☐ 7 pieces 5" × 40"

PIECE THE STRIPS

Lay out the strips you have cut from the print fabrics and figure out which strips need to be sewn together to make the strips 48″ wide. Using a ¼″ seam allowance, sew the smaller strips together so they are all at least 48″ wide. Make sure you have 27 strips 2½″ × 48″, and press seams open.

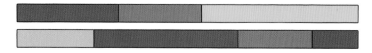

SEW THE THROW

To sew this throw, follow Sew the Throw, Steps 1–9, for *Simple Throw* (pages 125-127). Instead of alternating blue and white strips, you will alternate solid purple and multicolored print strips, as shown in the project photo (page 129) and Step 4.

1. The first strip will be solid purple. After you pin it on, roll up the fleece as for the simple throw. Sew the strip to the backing ¼″ from the edge, leaving the pins in place.

2. Unroll, add a multicolored strip, and sew the strips to the backing ¼″ from their edges.

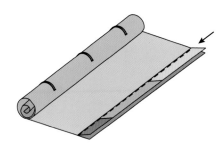

3. Continue with the strips as for *Simple Throw.*

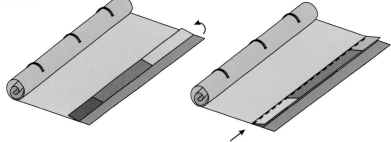

4. Alternate purple and multicolored strips in the following sequence:

Purple ⇨ 3 colored strips ⇨ Purple ⇨ 2 colored strips ⇨ Purple ⇨ 1 colored strip ⇨ Purple ⇨ 2 colored strips ⇨ and so on

> **Do you see the order?**

P ⇨ 3	P ⇨ 2	P ⇨ 1	P ⇨ 2	P ⇨ 3	P ⇨ 2	P ⇨ 1	P ⇨ 2	P ⇨ 3
P, C, C, C	P, C, C	P, C	P, C, C	P, C, C, C	P, C, C	P, C	P, C, C	P, C, C, C

Remember to sew from the opposite side of the throw with each new strip.

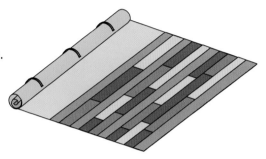

5. Once you've sewn the last strip on, flip it over and sew its final edge flat to the backing.

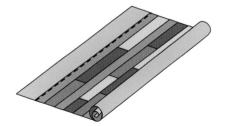

6. Spread the throw out fully on the floor. Using a yardstick and chalk, mark a straight line along each edge of the quilt and trim the edges even, as shown in *Simple Throw* (Sew the Throw, Step 9, page 127). Also trim extra fleece from the end.

BIND THE THROW

To bind the throw, follow Bind the Throw, Steps 1–9 (page 128), for *Simple Throw*.

zippered tote

This tote is the most complicated project in the book. But it's also one of the most rewarding, because it looks really good when you're done. It's a great project to do with a more experienced sewist who can help you with all of the different steps. Sophie couldn't believe the way it came together, because it looks so crazy while you're sewing. You can sew this tote without a zipper if you want to make it a little easier.

Finished size: 16″ wide × 18″ high × 5″ deep

MATERIALS

- ☐ 1 piece of upholstery vinyl 19″ × 38″

- ☐ 1 yard of lining fabric

- ☐ 22″ zipper (for optional zipper closure)

- ☐ Purchased handles and ¼ yard of 1″-wide nylon webbing for tabs *or* 1½–2 yards of 1″-wide nylon webbing for web handles

- ☐ Matching thread

TOOLS AND SUPPLIES

- ☐ Sewing machine

- ☐ Scissors or rotary cutter and mat

- ☐ Iron

- ☐ Straight pins

- ☐ Chalk or marking pen

- ☐ Binder clips or paper clips

CUTTING

From lining fabric, cut:

- ☐ 1 piece 18½″ × 37½″ for the lining

- ☐ 1 piece 8″ × 10″ for the pocket

- ☐ 2 zipper casings 5″ × 20″ (if adding the zipper closure)

- ☐ 1 zipper tab 1¾″ × 4½″ (if adding a zipper closure)

Sophie Says...

The tote bag is the hardest project in this book. There are so many steps. It looks really good when it's done, though. The part where you turn the bag inside out might seem a little bit weird, but it works! When you're making it, you can't tell how it's going to turn out. It's a lot easier if you don't make it with the zipper.

Sewing with vinyl is a little bit different than sewing with cotton or other types of fabric. Holes from pinning or sewing show in vinyl. So instead of pinning pieces together, we used binder clips. It's kind of fun to use the binder clips because it's different.

We used ready-made handles. You can also use regular webbing instead. Make sure the handles are even on both sides, or it will feel awkward when you carry it.

Tip

Vinyl sometimes sticks to sewing machine feet, making it hard to feed through. If you have a roller foot for your sewing machine, it will make sewing the vinyl easier. This special foot has a little roller that helps to feed the sticky vinyl through. If you don't have a roller foot, you can temporarily put masking tape on the area of the vinyl you'll be sewing to keep it from sticking. But be careful not to sew the tape into the bag, and be sure to take it off right away.

SEWING
Optional zipper top

If you want to a have a zipper at the top of the bag, follow the directions on this page. If you want the bag to have an open top, go directly to Make the Lining (page 135).

1. Fold 1 zipper casing in half lengthwise with wrong sides together. Press. Open up the casing, and fold the raw edges in until they meet the center crease. Press.

2. Fold in the short ends ¼", and press.

3. Repeat Steps 1 and 2 for the other casing.

4. Pin 1 long edge of the zipper to the inside of a casing. Tuck a raw end of the zipper tape down toward the fold as shown. It will then be covered when the casing is folded closed. The other end of the zipper will extend past the casing.

A zippered top keeps the tote contents safe and dry.

5. Fold the casing over the zipper tape, leaving the teeth showing. Topstitch around all 4 sides. When you get to the tucked-under end, take your foot off the foot pedal. Make the topstitching on the end by turning the hand wheel by hand, adjusting the casing as needed so you don't accidentally hit the zipper teeth and break the needle.

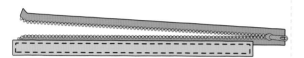

6. Repeat Steps 4 and 5 using the other casing to cover the second side of the zipper.

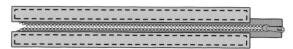

7. Press all 4 raw edges of the zipper tab in ¼˝.

8. Fold the tab in half, with wrong sides together. Slide it over the last ½˝ of the extended zipper end. Topstitch around all 4 sides of the tab. Set the zipper aside to be sewn into the lining later.

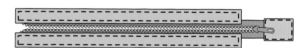

Make the lining

1. With right sides together, fold the fabric for the pocket in half to make a 5˝ × 8˝ rectangle. Press.

2. Stitch along 1 of the short ends and 1 open long side of the rectangle. Turn right side out.

3. Fold in the raw (unsewn) edge by ¼˝. Press it closed.

4. Using a marking pen or chalk, mark 2 points 3″ from the top edge of the lining. The first point should be 6″ from the side of the lining. The other should be about 12½″–13½″ from the same edge, depending on how careful you were with seam allowances on the pocket.

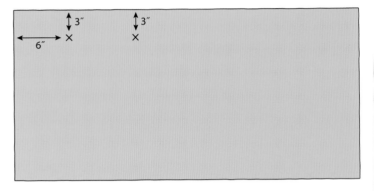

5. Using these marks as guides, pin the pocket with the folded edge up, and each of the top corners lining up with the marks.

6. Topstitch carefully around the sides and bottom of the pocket as close to the edge as you can. Be sure to backtack the first and last stitches as you sew, so they don't pull out with use.

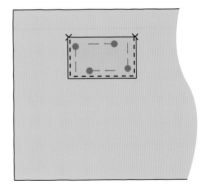

7. If you would like the pocket to hold a pen or pencil, stitch a vertical line 1½˝ from 1 side of the pocket.

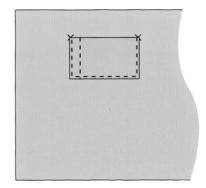

8. If you did not prepare the optional zipper, skip to Step 9. If you did prepare the zipper and casing, fold the lining in half, right sides together, with the 18½˝ sides matching. Mark the center. Fold in half again and mark the center. You will now have 3 marks across the top. Open the lining flat with the right side up. Mark the center of the length of the zipper. Unzip the zipper and pin each half centered on 1 side of the lining, with the edge of the casing 1¼˝ below the top edge of the lining (see below). Stitch over the top edge of the previous topstitching. The bottom edge along the zipper teeth is left free.

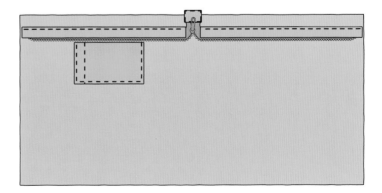

9. Fold the lining in half with right sides together, and pin. Using a ¼˝ seam allowance, stitch along the side, and continue along the bottom as shown. Leave an 8˝ gap at the bottom of the lining so you'll be able to turn the bag right side out when you're done.

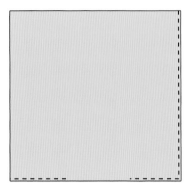

10. This lining and the outside bag have gussets at the bottom corners to make a flat bottom. Make a gusset by folding the bottom corner of the lining into a triangle as shown. Make sure the side and bottom seams are lined up in the center of the triangle. Mark a line where the triangle is 5˝ wide. Sew on the marked line to make the gusset.

11. Leaving a ½˝ seam allowance, trim the triangle off the gusset.

12. Repeat Steps 10 and 11 for the other corner.

Sew the outside bag

1. Fold the vinyl in half widthwise to measure 19″ × 19″, with the fold at the bottom. Line up the top corners, and secure them with the clips.

2. Using a ½″ seam allowance, sew the sides.

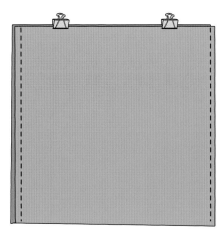

3. Make the gussets as you did in Steps 10 and 11 for the lining.

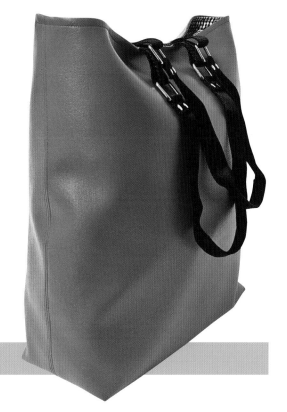

Put the bag together

1. Keep the vinyl layer of the bag turned right side out. Mark the center of each side of the bag.

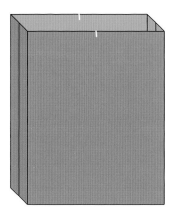

2. Center the handles (or the tabs that will attach the ready-made handles) on each side of the bag. Position the handles so they hang down on the outside of the bag and the ends stick up slightly above the top edge of the bag. Adjust how far from the center each handle should be to make them a comfortable fit on your shoulder. Clip the handles on each side of the bag.

3. Make sure the vinyl bag is right side out, with the handles hanging down on the outside. Make sure the lining is right side in, with the pocket on the inside. Then slip the vinyl bag inside the lining. This will seem very odd because the handles are between lining and the vinyl, and the lining is on the outside.

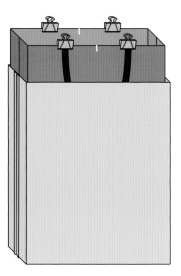

4. Align the top edges of the lining and vinyl, and clip them together. Sew around the top about ⅛″ from the edge.

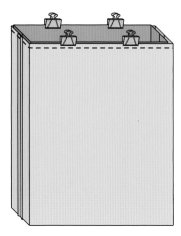

5. Lift the lining up over the tote so the unsewn gap in the lining is at the top. Fold the bottom unsewn edges in ¼", and pin them together. Topstitch across.

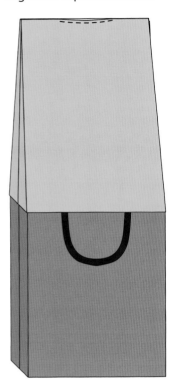

6. Slide the lining inside the tote. Finger press the top edge, where the lining and vinyl are joined, to make a sharp crease. Topstitch around the opening ¼" from the top.

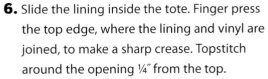

RESOURCES

Fabric

There are three main places to buy fabric: national chain stores, independent quilt shops, and online retailers.

National chain stores These are large stores like Hancock Fabrics and Jo-Ann Fabric and Craft Stores. They have lots of different fabrics and accessories, and they're easy to find in most communities. If you need help and advice, some of the people working there may sew, but not all are experienced sewists. Sometimes it's too crowded to get personal advice on a project. Be aware that in general, chain stores do not carry the best-quality quilting cottons.

Independent quilt shops There are thousands of independent quilt shops across the United States and the world. Each one sells different styles of fabric. Some may have cuddle fleece, while others may have wool or home dec fabric. They all have quilting cotton, but the styles really vary from store to store. Some have more traditional fabrics and others have bold, graphic prints. You will find the best quality of fabric at these stores. That's why the prices are usually a bit higher than at national chains. One of the best things about independent quilt shops is that almost everyone who works there is a great sewist! If you buy fabric there, they will often give you helpful advice. Most offer classes for quilting, and some offer classes for other kinds of projects as well.

Online retailers Some online retailers also have shops you can visit if you live nearby. But most sell only through the Internet. It's very convenient to buy from online shops, but you can't tell exactly what color a fabric will be. You don't get to touch it, feel the weight of the fabric, or see the quality. However, online shopping is great if you don't live near a good fabric store. You do usually have to pay extra for shipping, and you can't get advice on projects.

Tools and Supplies

C&T Publishing, FunStitch Studio, and Stash Books   ctpub.com
A huge array of books on sewing, crafting, and quilting

Clover   clover-usa.com
This Japanese company makes outstanding craft supplies. Many national chain stores sell Clover supplies but you can also find them online.

Dritz   dritz.com
A lot of different sewing supplies, including elastic, D-rings, bicycle clips for quilting, and other accessories. You can find Dritz products in stores or online.

Renaissance Ribbons
renaissanceribbons.com
By far the best selection of beautiful ribbons

Victorinox Swiss Army Inc.   swissarmy.com
Victorinox Performance-Shield Cut Resistant Glove. Available in extra small for kids' hands.

Therm O Web   thermowebonline.com

Pellon   pellonideas.com
Both Therm O Web and Pellon sell laminating sheets, also known as iron-on vinyl. Laminating sheets are also available where sewing supplies are sold.

Weeks Dye Works   weeksdyeworks.com
Hand-dyed wools, linens, and embroidery floss

about the authors

Sophie Kerr grew up sewing with her parents, Weeks Ringle and Bill Kerr. When not at school or hanging out with friends, Sophie also plays soccer, skateboards, sings in a choir, cycles long distances with her parents, and loves all things *Peanuts*, especially Snoopy.

Weeks and Bill are co-founders of Modern Quilt Studio and have been making modern quilts since 1999. They are the authors of *The Modern Quilt Workshop*, the first book ever published on modern quilting, as well as *Quiltmaker's Color Workshop*, *Quilts Made Modern*, and *Transparency Quilts*. In 2011 they launched *Modern Quilts Illustrated*, the first magazine dedicated exclusively to modern quilting, which is sold worldwide.

Weeks teaches a class on designing modern quilts at Craftsy.com and has written articles about modern quilting for *American Patchwork & Quilting*, *American Quilter*, *Quilts Japan*, and *American Quilt Retailer*. When he's not working in the studio, Bill is a professor and head of the art department at Dominican University in River Forest, Illinois. Sophie, Weeks, Bill, and their cat, Mies, live in Oak Park, Illinois.